Thomas Day

The Letters of Marius

Reflections upon the Peace, the East-India Bill and the Present Crisis.

Fourth Edition

Thomas Day

The Letters of Marius
Reflections upon the Peace, the East-India Bill and the Present Crisis. Fourth Edition

ISBN/EAN: 9783744715669

Printed in Europe, USA, Canada, Australia, Japan

Cover: Foto ©Suzi / pixelio.de

More available books at **www.hansebooks.com**

THE

LETTERS OF MARIUS:

OR,

REFLECTIONS

UPON THE

PEACE,

THE

EAST-INDIA BILL,

AND THE

PRESENT CRISIS;

By THOMAS DAY, Eſq.

———— Non ante revellar,
Exanimem quam te complectar, Roma, tuumque
Nomen libertas, et inanem proſequar umbram.

FOURTH EDITION,

LONDON:

PRINTED FOR J. STOCKDALE,
OPPOSITE BURLINGTON HOUSE, PICCADILLY.
MDCCLXXXIV.

ADVERTISEMENT.

IT is neceſſary to give a reaſon why the following reflections are publiſhed under the fictitious name of MARIUS. They were originally intended to be printed in the public papers, and the firſt five letters were written before the author changed his plan. But the bulk into which they inſenſibly ſwelled, made them ſeem more adapted to the form under which they now appear: at the ſame time neither the urgency of the preſent criſis, nor the variety of ſubjects to be treated, allowed him to melt them down anew, and give them the uniformity of a continued eſſay. The neceſſity of immediately preſenting ſuch ſentiments as theſe, if they are preſented at all, to the public, has alſo induced the author to publiſh with a precipitation, which he would otherwiſe diſapprove.

THE

THE

LETTERS OF MARIUS,
&c.

LETTER I.

To Dr. J E B B.

S I R,

IF, in the moſt dangerous criſis, the conſul
Varro was thought to deſerve the thanks
of the Roman people whoſe very exiſtence he
had endangered, merely, " quod non deſperâſ-
ſet de republicâ," with what honours ſhould
the Engliſh nation exalt your name?——In the
midſt of dangers, ſo much the more formidable
as the internal corruption of any ſtate is more
to be feared than every external ſhock, your
uniform conduct has been to animate by your

B   example,

example, and to enlighten by your underſtanding, the wavering aud dejected minds of your countrymen. While this has uniformly been your public conduct, your private example ſeems deſtined to reſcue the injured term of Patriotiſm from the unmerited ridicule which had been brought upon it by the treachery of its pretended friends.

While every raſh adventurer, while every ruined libertine, could find a beneficial trade in duping the credulity of the people; while every broken author, gambler, pimp, or paraſite, when deprived of the hope of ſubſiſting by his honeſt induſtry, could promiſe himſelf a decent ſubſiſtence, if not the enjoyment of his favourite vices, by enliſting himſelf under the banners of the popular cauſe, it was no wonder that cauſe ſhould be ſo often abandoned and betrayed as we have ſeen it. But, if we lament the miſapplication of the public confidence, in a variety of inſtances, we muſt, at leaſt, allow that the evil has not been unproductive of utility. There is a limit beyond which credulity itſelf will not ſubmit to be deceived; and that limit the Engliſh people have happily attained. I have not yet heard that the political qualms of Lord North againſt ſecret influence, and the harangues of Mr. Fox in favour of a parliamentary

majority,

majority, have made a fingle profelyte out of
their own virtuous houfe. There, indeed, a
faving faith, according to the true orthodox
form of " Credo quia impoffibile," has given a
wonderful efficacy to the word ; and many a
ftubborn infidel, who would not have believed
" even though one had rifen from the dead,"
has already yielded to the bare promife of a
fhower of manna, or a fecond miracle of the
loaves and fifhes. But with the body of the
people the cafe is widely different. They have
learned to attend to the ftubborn voice of facts,
as well as to the more foothing notes of oratori-
cal perfuafion. They demand a certain confiftency of life and manners, the delicate colouring of private honefty and integrity, to fill
up the flowing outline of public profeffion,
and to make it worthy of a people's admiration.
This, fir, is what envy itfelf will not deny to
be your undifputed claim. The Englifh people, therefore, receive you as their undoubted
benefactor, and, whatever may be the confequence of your exertions, allow you all the
glory which is due to the purity and difintereftednefs of your intentions.

But it is not enough, in public contefts, to
have gained the cleareft praife of integrity, unlefs we can add to it that of difcretion and

judg-

judgment. Cato expiated, within the walls of Utica, the ill-timed deference which he had ſhewn to Scipio; and Cicero paid with his blood the price of his fond idolatry of Octavius. The Engliſh people, that have been always doomed to expiate either the treachery or the puſillanimity of their leaders, will find it difficult to determine which of theſe qualities has produced the greateſt miſchief. While the one has given up all their rights at the very moment when they might have been eſtabliſhed, the other has repeatedly checked them in their moſt ſuccefsful career, with ideal difficulties, and delays, which are always friendly to uſurpation as they are dangerous to liberty.

Never did this appear more evident than in the year 1779, which gave birth to the aſſociations of the people. Wearied out at that time with the abſurd conduct of an unjuſt war, into which they had been betrayed by every ſpecies of falſehood and miſrepreſentation, they turned their eyes, with a gratitude little ſhort of adoration, upon that ſudden light which unexpectedly roſe upon their darkened horizon. Nor can it be doubted, that it was much leſs the people who were then wanting to their own cauſe, than that they were, as uſual, deſerted by their leaders. A few, a very few diſintereſted men, among whom

whom it will ever be your praife to have been the foremoft, ftood forth, and called the public attention to the radical and inveterate corruptions of the conftitution. " In vain," faid they to that body of the gentry and nobility which fupported the caufe of oppofition, " do you attempt to palliate, or temporize with your difeafe. In vain do you diftract the attention of the people upon the trifling details of their government, and cheat them with idle vifions of œconomical reforms. Were the public miferies occafioned either by accidental incapacity, or accidental misfortune, we might hope for relief from time, and fpare ourfelves the trouble of exertion ; but, where a long unbroken feries of events has been unfolded, all tending to the fame end, and that end the depreffion of the people and the deftruction of their rights, it calls for all our vigilance and virtue. Even now, the meafure of our wrongs is full ; nor have we any remaining hope but from courage founded upon defpair. For whom will ye invoke in this extremity of diftrefs, but yourfelves? —Will ye prefer your petitions to the throne which has fo often fpurned, fo often rejected them ; and hope that a fovereign will undertake the patronage of public freedom, when it is no longer defended by the fpirit of a nation ?

Hiftory

Hiftory, indeed, commemorates fovereigns who have practifed the virtues and the philofophy of private life, who have loved their friends, pardoned their enemies, and endured the approach of truth ; fome have even defcended from their thrones, and fought for happinefs in obfcurity : but the example is yet wanting of a prince who has loft an opportunity of increafing his power, or refigned the ufurpations of his predeceffors.

" But according to the principles of the Englifh conflitution, you have little either to hope or to fear from the private qualities of a fovereign : or, rather, by an happy fiction which makes every minifter that fhares the executive power anfwerable for his own omiffions, the prince may enjoy all the reverence of his virtues, while his name is never compromifed by the guilty projects of ambition. But however implicitly we may admit the maxim, That a king can do no wrong, flattery itfelf has never yet applied it to his fervants ; and fhould we appeal to experience, it may perhaps be doubted whether the impeccability of the fovereign is not compenfated by a contrary quality in his minifters. Nothing then remains but that ye ufe the only check which the conftitution has provided, and order your reprefentatives to impeach the guilty
authors

authors of your miseries. But, alas! such is
the peculiar unhappiness of our situation, that
those whom we should apply to for redress are
the very authors of our misfortunes. For is
there a single minister, that has insulted the
patience or eluded the vengeance of the people,
that is not fenced in by a majority of those who
call themselves your representatives? What
measure has been so stigmatized by public de-
testation, so openly inimical to the liberties and
interests of a free people, as not to be sanctified
by a majority of that honourable house? If
we take their whole successive conduct, from
their open and indecent attacks upon the dear-
est privileges of the people in the Middlesex
election, down to their premeditated invasion
of the American rights, and all the subsequent
horrors of the civil war in which we are now
engaged, is there a single action worthy of the
generosity, greatness, or understanding of the
English people?—Nor do we found our opinion
upon vague surmize or uncertain conjecture.
Whatever undoubted virtue and ability this
country can boast in its public councils, whatever characters of superior lustre, have all combined in vain to stem the torrent; and they
now appeal from the venal votes of a corrupt
majority to the sober and unbiassed suffrages of
the

the people. Who can doubt the integrity, the difintereftednefs, more than the talents of a Fox, and Burke? And when you behold the fruitlefs efforts of men like thefe, to point their country's thunders at the head of its implacable foe, and hear them publicly affert that wifdom and ability alike are vain; that all the former fpirit of our parliament is evaporated, and has left nothing behind but blind fervility to a mi- nifter, can we hefitate to admit the fatal truth?—No! could there yet remain a doubt, we feel it in the degradation of our country, and the increafing mifery of its inhabitants.——Roufe then, if ever, ye laft remaining hopes of liberty, and unite for its defence!"

MARIUS.

LET-

LETTER II.

To Dr. JEBB.

SIR

WHOEVER would write adequately concerning public affairs, muſt not confine his attention to the preſent moment, but muſt include a ſeries of paſt events, as neceſſary to eſtabliſh his opinions both of the preſent and the future. With this intention, I recurred, in my laſt letter, to the year 1779, and gave a ſummary of what was then addreſſed to the people, by thoſe who coincided in your ſentiments of the cauſe of national grievances : I ſhall now drop the third perſon, and proceed, in my own, to ſubmit to the judgment of the public the arguments in favour of correcting the repreſentation of the people which were then uſed; and which are now neceſſary to be remembered, if we wiſh for any adequate remedy to the evils which ſurround us.

Hiſtory furniſhes us with a variety of forms in which the human ſpecies have exiſted under

C

different

different modifications both of tyranny and freedom. Indeed, every thing is fo mixed in human affairs, that it is perhaps impoffible to produce an inftance of any government which is
purely either the one, or the other. Scarcely
any arbitrary government exifts, which is not
limited in its exceffes, either by the prejudices
of manners or religion; fcarcely any free one
which does not contain within itfelf the feeds
of its own future deftruction. This confideration has given wonderful fcope to the ingenuity of thofe who wifh to confound the underftandings of men, and to mifreprefent the plaineft
facts. You that, for the fake of alleviating the
real miferies of your fellow-creatures, are continually obliged to confider thofe miferies in
their moft hideous forms, know that nothing
is more difficult than to define the precife boun-
daries of health and difeafe : yet the wildeft
fceptic will not deny that thefe ideas have a real
exiftence, and that it is the effential intereft of
man to inveftigate them with all the accuracy
he poffeffes.

In politics, it muft be confeffed, we can
fcarcely proceed a ftep, without finding equal
caufe to lament the imperfect nature of paft
experience, and the yet more imperfect manner
in which it is recorded. But in what fcience,

unlefs

unlefs it be pure mathematics, can we pretend
to certainty, or even accuracy? The conduct
of life, therefore, muft either be permitted to
probability, or left to fluctuate at random.
And, if we obferve the common behaviour of
our fellow-creatures, we muft acknowledge that
they do not fo much fuffer from the fcantinefs
of their materials, as from a want of diligence
and judgment in application of them.

Without involving myfelf, therefore, in all
the fubtleties of metaphyfical diftinctions, I fhall
fimply obferve, that one common fact is univer-
fally found in every free government; a public
and legal method, by which the fpirit of the
nation at large may declare itfelf to its governors, and either confirm or alter the courfe of
meafures. Wherever we turn our eyes, I affert
that this circumftance has been always found to
accompany public liberty, and to meafure its
extent and duration: nor is there a fingle example, in hiftory, of any country that has not
been enflaved the very moment when it fuffered either violence or cajolery to deprive it
of this ineftimable privilege.

Nor will it, perhaps, be lofs of time, if I
paufe here to anfwer a common fophifm which I
have remarked in all the writers on the other fide
of the queftion. Government, they, indeed, al-

C 2   low

low to be a truft, and to be exercifed for the good
of the people; but as to the actual confent and
will of the people themfelves, they place it entirely out of the queftion. They felect, with
wonderful ingenuity and perfeverance, all the inftances of popular fury, caprice, and ingratitude,
which they can find in hiftory, to contraft them
with the moft favourable periods of arbitrary government; and then they triumphantly afk, whether all thefe outrages and excufes compofe freedom, while juftice, order, and humanity as naturally conftitute fervitude. But this is either a
wilful, or involuntary confufion of ideas. There
can be no doubt but there are periods in the life
of every individual, when it might be more con-
ducive to his intereft to be under the controul of
a difcreet friend, than abandoned to the weaknefs
and inexperience of his own judgment. No
doubt, but there are many inftances in which you
could extend the benefits of the medical art, were
you able to enforce your precepts of regimen and
exercife by a falutary degree of reftraint; but
will any one argue fo inaccurately as, for that
reafon, to affert, that men would become more
free by being fubjected to the arbitrary will of a
phyfician, in all that concerned their health;
more efpecially, were one of his fubalterns daily

to

to feel their pulfe, in order to determine the al-
terations which took place ?

In truth, nothing can be more inaccurate than
to produce the mifchiefs which may fometimes
arife from liberty, or the advantages which may
accidentally refult from flavery, as a reafon for
confounding the ideas. The man is certainly
more free than the child, although in many inftances it might be for his advantage ftill to trem-
ble at the ferula ; and the American favage, even
while he is perifhing for hunger in his native
woods, than the beft-fed negro of the iflands.
But to argue with any regard for accuracy or
logic, the battery fhould be changed ; and it muft
be maintained, that it is really more for the intereft
of any nation to abandon its claim to liberty, than
to fubmit to the inconveniences of preferving it.
This is the fuppofition which, under a variety of
difguifes, has been frequently obtruded upon the
prefs ; and therefore I will beftow fome confideration upon it, that I may not be afterwards in-
terrupted in the progrefs of thefe letters.

I have often thought it a wonderful fallacy of
fome divines to depreciate human reafon in order
to exalt religion : for, unlefs that religion be im-
parted by particular infpiration to every individual,
what other method is there of eftablifhing it,
than proofs adapted to his reafon ? The more,

there-.

therefore, you convince him of the weaknefs and fallibility of that faculty, the more you muft incline him, were he confiftent, to doubt his power of judging concerning the particular evidence you propofe. But this fallacy does not feem to be confined to the venerable order of the clergy. Politicians practife it at leaft with equal fuccefs, when they defcant upon the blindnefs and ignorance of, what they call, the multitude. The paffions of mankind, they tell you, are fo ftrong, and their reafoning powers fo weak, that nothing but anarchy and confufion can refult from their being permitted to govern themfelves. What then is the remedy? Would one not expect that they would bring fome god or angel down to take the management of affairs upon himfelf, and atone for human imperfections? But here they are inferior to their friends the clergy. Inftead of this device, they have only the very contemptible one of felecting a fmall part of the fpecies, who are not only to govern themfelves, but all the reft. So that this unavoidable contradiction arifes from the fuppofition ; mankind are totally incapable of governing themfelves, yet they are not only capable of governing themfelves, but millions of others at the fame time. Nor is it poffible to avoid this confequence, by afferting that certain individuals excel in prudence

dence and wifdom, and therefore are by nature adapted for this purpofe : for what are the marks that diftinguifh thefe individuals, and who is to judge of their authenticity ? If the bulk of mankind is too grofs and blind to decide concerning this fuperior excellence, it muft be fome-body elfe that determines for it. But how are we to diftinguifh thefe few, that, like the Venetian electors, are to chufe for all the reft ; and that without a previous election, or even a form of ballot ? If it be merely the few, in oppofition to the many, it will be poffible to divide the largeft number till you reduce it to the fmalleft ; but it is an original idea to fuppofe that ignorance and ftupidity may be divided and fub-divided, till they become knowledge and underftanding.

But here is the general fallacy both of divines and politicians : both begin by teaching you to diftruft yourfelf, and addrefs themfelves, if I may ufe the expreffion, to the hypocondriacifm of human nature. When their reprefentations have fucceeded to a certain degree, they give you to underftand that the only cure for all your evils is to adopt their own particular fyftem either of faith or government. What is orthodoxy, true religion, and the will of heaven, on the one fide ; or herefy, fchifm, and idolatry on the other ? — The particular opinions which
every

every divine holds forth, or which he chufes to condemn.——In the words of Hudibras,

" What makes all doctrines plain and clear ?
" About two hundred pounds a year."

Thus if you demand of the politician what is order, good government, and political wifdom? Will he not anfwer, if he fpeak truth, the fub- miffion of mankind to the particular opinions which I entertain, or which I am paid for diffe- minating.—If, on the contrary, what is rebelli- on, faction, fedition, treafon ?—Different degrees of the opinions which either my avarice or am- bition would prove falfe. But fhould you prefs him further, he muft be compelled either to ad- mit the general right of all the fpecies to judge as well as act for themfelves, or elfe to involve himfelf in inextricable contradictions.

M A R I U S.

LETTER

LETTER III.

To Dr. J E B B.

SIR

HE that builds, from caprice or vanity, may content himfelf with the flimfy decorations and patch-work ornaments of modern tafte. However weak may be the foundations, however frail the materials, the edifice will be the wonder of a day, and may then unheeded crumble into ruins. Had I intended thefe papers to be the auxiliaries of party, or the inftruments of private ambition, I had haftened to feize the perifhable topic of the hour, before it gave place to the next new object of fafhionable purfuit and wonder. But however vain may be the attempt, however inadequate my ambition, I have propofed to myfelf an higher object: I aim at placing that folid information before the public, which may guide their judgment, and direct their conduct. I fhall too foon be obliged to quit the peaceful walks of fpeculation for the crooked and dangerous labyrinths of modern ftatefmen and politicians.

However

However ftrong may be the arguments in favour of political liberty which are produced by
the underftanding alone, thofe which are derived
from experience will give them additional force.

Man is forbidden by the laws of his orga-
nization to afpire at immortality ; yet why fhould
diffolution be equally the fate of every human inftitution? May we not conceive a fociety eftablifhed on
fuch a bafis, as to brave the fhocks of time ; and to
remain, like the feveral fpecies of the animal
world, immortal and incorruptible, though compofed of a thoufand perifhable generations ?

Alas! it will be anfwered, human inftitutions,
though at longer intervals, are equally mortal
with the individuals that compofe them. To raife
an eternal fabric, with materials that are in a continual ftate of fluctuation and decay, is a vainer
attempt than "to build a city and a tower whofe
top may reach unto Heaven."

What government is recorded, within the annals of time, fo wifely framed, fo folidly eftablifhed, as not to have degenerated into tyranny;
and what tyranny that has not foon been overturn-
ed, by relaxing all the fprings of national defence,
and enfeebling the community in order to en-
flave it ? Nay, the very inftitutions of Heaven itfelf, the inftant they were entrufted to human
paffions for their fupport, have fcarcely met
with

with a different fate, or conftituted an exception.
The firft apoftles of chriftianity were mild and
lowly, like the founder of their faith. They addreffed themfelves to the reafon of men, and pro-
pagated their religion by perfuafion. They ab-
jured the luxuries and the enjoyments of fenfe ;
they fubmitted to every infult; they refufed the
offered benefits of their friends, and deprecated,
only by prayers and bleffings, the malice of their
enemies. But mark the change! The inftant a
royal convert has given the clergy entrance to a
court, they abjure every principle of their religion.
Then we lofe fight of a fuffering, and begin the
æra of a triumphant church. The immediate
fucceffors of fifhermen and mechanics confent to
be cloathed in purple and fcarlet, to wallow in all
the fenfualities of the moft abandoned age and
country, and to difgrace the fimplicity of the moft
fpiritual religion, by the rites and ceremonies of
the groffeft. The power of confulting about the
interpretation of the articles of their religion,
which was exprefily given to the whole body of
chriftians, is, in a fhort time, monopolized by
the clergy; and the power of chufing their paf-
tors and bifhops, a right equally deducible from
equity, hiftory, reafon, and the fcriptures, taken
from the laity, and fhared between the hierarchy
and the civil power. And this fyftem of practice

and

and belief, fo grofsly adulterated, fo totally un-
like the original, is called Chriftianity, and enforced by racks, and flames, and gibbets ; the
antient fupporters of civil, and now the welcome
auxiliaries of ecclefiaftical power. What may we
fuppofe would have been the ftate of chriftianity
at the prefent hour, had not the daring and original genius of Luther reduced it fomething nearer
to its original principles, in the fixteenth century?
What may we fuppofe will be its ftate in the
twentieth, fhould no new Luther arife to teach
our clergy the diftance between the houfe of the
Lord and the courts of princes, the difference between the fervice of God and mammon?

But I forefee that fome of my readers may
here exclaim, All this may be true, but what is it
to the purpofe? You are writing upon government and political liberty, why then deviate to
the abufes and corruptions of chriftianity?—Becaufe the hiftory of chriftianity, a perfect and
recorded fucceffion of facts, which every man
may confider at his leifure, is the beft illuftration
in the univerfe of the fubject on which I am
writing. Becaufe, if neither the immediate doctrines of Heaven itfelf, nor its pofitive commands,
have been able to preferve even a chriftian clergy
from every corruption which can grow upon the
felfifh paffions, what are we to expect will be the

fate

fate of inftitutions merely human, if once abandoned to the avarice, ambition, and indolence of
thofe who have an equal intereft to pervert them ?
· While, therefore, I plead the caufe of truth,
and defend the intereft of the human fpecies, the
wider my range, the more extenfive my obfervations, the greater will be the force of thofe con-
clufions which I fhall eftablifh upon the united
evidence of fpeculation, reafon, and practical experience.

The favourers of a parliamentary reform have
been repeatedly attacked with all the virulence of
anonymous felfifhnefs and malevolence. They
are "idle fpeculatifts, nurfed in the gloom of
folitude and ignorance," " men of defpicable
abilities," " of neither fortune or confequence,"
" actuated by private intereft and malevolence,"
and an hundred other characters equally liberal
and candid.—If they indeed be all this, and the
fubftance of a thoufand other invectives which
have been lavifhed upon them, no doubt from the
pureft motives, they certainly deferve the contempt
of all their countrymen. But let the matter be
brought fairly to iffue before that public which is
appealed to. Marius is the laft and meaneft of
that body. Should he be foiled, an hundred
abler champions are ready to enter the field, and
the caufe which he maintains will receive no difgrace

difgrace from the weaknefs of its defender. But, fhould the arguments which he adduces remain unconfuted, what will the public think of the courage of his adverfaries, or of the juftice of their, caufe?

   " Each fearlefs hero dares an hundred foes,
   " While the feaft lafts, and while the goblet flows;
   " But who to meet one martial man is found,
   " When the fight rages, and the flames furround?"

                     POPE's ILIAD.

Some of thefe gentlemen are famous for their metaphyfical acutenefs. Let them therefore defcend into the field, and prove the falfity of the principles which I have laid down. If they can be confuted, it will fave me the trouble of proceeding in my courfe, and profecuting an enquiry commenced under fuch inaufpicious omens. Or, as they fometimes affect to defpife fpeculation, and feem to imagine that all the underftanding of the world is comprized in the dull routine of parliamentary bufinefs and oppofition dinners, let them difprove this practical maxim upon which I reft the merits of the caufe, " That there is no inftance of any body of men which have not abufed whatever trufts were repofed in them, to the vileft purpofes of felfifhnefs, the inftant they were not acted upon by fome external force which kept them true to the purpofes of their inftitution.".

                     Should

Should these points either not be denied, or being denied should not be adequately disproved by argument, I will take the liberty of stating the manner in which I intend to apply my principles; and the conclusion I shall attempt to establish.

In the first place, it is my opinion, as has been repeatedly affirmed by a majority of the nation, that the present House of Commons is no representation of the English people.

And this, I imagine, will be the more easily conceived even by my adversaries, as many of them; rather than grant the force of any argument in favour of public liberty, have chosen to deny that representation was any part of the English constitution.

In the second place, I assert, that, if the present House of Commons does not really represent the people, the people have no constitutional method of either effectually enforcing or opposing public measures.

In the third place, I will take the liberty of examining the conduct of those who are called the representatives of the people, particularly in respect to the celebrated East-India business.

And should I succeed in establishing the principles which I have here advanced, I shall submit it to the understanding of my countrymen, whether, while they are so tremblingly alive to the rights of

sovereigns

fovereigns and minifters, it does not become them to have fome regard for their own.

I have addreffed thefe letters to you, fir, becaufe I think the efteem and gratitude of the public conftitute the fit reward of virtuous actions. No one has exerted himfelf more ftrenuoufly, more difintereftedly, more uniformly. While Mr. ——— appeared the champion of the people and their rights, you reverenced him with a zeal which I never thought his conduct deferved. But it is the cleareft proof of your own integrity, that you have been able to relinquifh thofe habitual delufions the inftant you could be convinced they were mifplaced. In refpect to the refolutions brought forward at the laft meeting of the quintuple alliance, I am convinced, they contain dangerous and falutary truths, little likely to be adopted by the indolence of this nation, but neceffary to influence their conduct, if they afpire to continue a free people. To place this fubject in the cleareft light, and to bring it home to the hearts and underftandings of my countrymen, is the only aim of

MARIUS.

LETTER IV.

Right Honourable the EARL of STAIR.

My LORD,

THERE is an ambition in the human
mind, which may at least be pardoned,
if not commended, of connecting itself with
every object of public esteem. Poets have ex-
hausted the comparison of the oak and ivy; and
your lordship is too well acquainted with poetry
as well as calculation, to need a reference to
the particular passages. I am contented for once
to be the subject of the allusion, and to have
it supposed that MARIUS would rise to notice
upon the blasts which spread your lordship's
fame.

In your last pamphlet, you express a wish
that the euthanasia of the English constitution
may be a mild despotism. Had such a senti-
ment proceeded from any of the common rep-
tiles that are engendered in the corruptions of
a court, we should have only said, " The crea-

ture's

ture's at his dirty work again," and paffed it over in filent contempt: but when it proceeds from a man, who, apparently retired from human affairs, fhrouds himfelf in his own integrity, and delivers oracular fayings from the precincts of confecrated groves, we furely muft be as much aftonifhed as the frighted heathen, that heard treachery recommended from the tripod of Apollo.

The public, my lord, have given you undoubted credit for the apparent zeal with which you oppofed the American war. Confidering the prejudices of your country, they allowed it to be no trifling effort. They even pardoned fome little advances towards Lord North *, in confideration of the fpirit with which you abufed the majority of the parliament and the reft of the adminiftration. But this was nothing more than had been already done by many of the moft diftinguifhed characters in the nation; nor

can

* " The noble lord has much in poffeffion, more in reverfion: happy in his family, happy in his fortune and abilities, with ftrong natural and focial affections, no one muft drink deeper of the bitter cup of national humiliation and ruin. In his public line of conduct I fee, or fancy that I fee, and in his alone, of all the ruthlefs minifterial tribe, fome twitches of remorfe,

fome

can we therefore allow you the full merit of your modeſt inſinuation: "It is the comfort, it is the glory of my life to have oppoſed, almoſt ſingly, in the beginning, that war, at the ſure conſequence and expence of all that has happened to me *."

Was your lordſhip ignorant, when you hazarded that aſſertion, that the American war had been openly oppoſed, not only by a conſiderable party in parliament, but by a numerous body of independent men in every quarter of the kingdom ? That petitions had been ſent from many of the trading towns and the counties of South Britain ?

The miniſterial writers of that ill-omened hour are full of menaces againſt the factious party at home that juſtified the reſiſtance of the Americans. They firſt, we are told, lighted up the flame of rebellion ; they afterwards gave new force to its half-extinguiſhed violence ; they dictated the reſolutions of congreſs, the march of Waſhing-

ſome recollections of the fair feelings of humanity, ſome ſweet drops of the milk of human kindneſs."

FACTS AND THEIR CONSEQUENCES, p. 26.

I heard it obſerved, when this paſſage was firſt publiſhed, that his lordſhip muſt have ſeen all this by ſecond ſight ; for not an Engliſhman could ever diſcover the leaſt of all theſe wonders.

* An argument to prove, that it is the indiſpenſable Duty, &c. by John, Earl of Stair, p. 24.

E 2

ton.

ton, the independence of America, and the eternal humiliation of their own country:

" They hated, they defpis'd, and they deftroy."

Does your lordfhip ferioufly believe that all
this feries of accufations relates to you alone?
That you were the only object of minifterial
hatred, of party rancour, of American gratitude? Or have you never yet heard the names
of Richmond, Chatham, Camden, and even of
Dr. Price?

" Me, me! adfum qui feci, in me convertite ferrum."

But, if you inveft yourfelf with this pre-emi-
nence, you fhould at leaft have fitted yourfelf to
fupport with dignity the part you voluntarily
affume. We can conceive Cato tearing out his
own bowels, or Brutus, with his laft breath,
complaining that heaven had abandoned the
caufe of virtue ; but we cannot fo eafily conceive
the laft of Romans carrying up an addrefs to
welcome the conqueror from the plains of Phar-
falia, and congratulating his triumphs over the
conftitution.

But this infinuation may perhaps be controverted by your lordfhip's friends: let us try
how far it can be brought home from the
evidence of your own writings. He that never
omits

omits an opportunity of casting contempt and ridicule upon every expedient, one alone excepted, may fairly be imagined to think more highly of that exception, and to prefer it to all the rest. Interest, as well as vanity, may find out more paths than one of arriving at its ends: and he is little acquainted with the world, who is ignorant that to degrade an enemy is often the same thing as to recommend a friend.

You have taken every opportunity, in the different tracts you have published, of expressing your contempt of all public characters, and of a great majority of the House of Commons. Let us hear your own words : " The happy counterpoise of the different parts of our constitution is destroyed ; all responsibility is made a jest ; for, backed by a majority, paid to support, and paid to applaud their measures, be they what they may, ministers gather the roses without the cares or the thorns of power ; and from the number and rank, and even fortunes of the corrupted, fashion and ton is given to the basest prostitutions of principles and of talents*."— Again : " Was indeed, as in the days of our ancestors, the fable believed, of a bargain and sale to the Devil for temporary honours and

* Facts and their Consequences, p. 25.

emoluments,

emoluments, I much fear that the *prince of darkness* would hold a majority in the British parliament †."—I have selected these from a variety of passages equally strong and pointed, because I think they must be allowed to convey a very unequivocal idea of your sentiments. But if ministers, if even parliaments, are so radically corrupted, it can be neither from ministers nor parliaments, such as they are at present, that the nation is to expect its safety. Wherever the prince of darkness may obtain a majority, I will answer for it he will never want a substitute to manage affairs in his behalf.

One only alternative therefore remains, unless the nation ought to be entirely passive under such a complicated weight of injuries and calamities : it may insist upon reforming the corruptions of its reprefentatives, or it may confent to abolish' representation altogether, and take shelter in what you feelingly call "a mild despotism."—Should the few remaining friends of their country's liberties, for such friends *may* even now remain, adopt the former part of the alternative, it appears to me no reflection upon their *hearts*, and but little upon their *heads*.

† Attempt to balance the Income and Expenditure of the State, p. 18.

The

The bounds of poſſibility are little known to the ordinary part of mankind. The few ſuperior minds that have enlarged them for the ſpecies, were looked upon at firſt as raſh adventurers, who were only accelerating their own deſtruction. If the opinions of mankind are forcibly altered by ſucceſs, it ariſes, I fear, leſs from juſtice than from vanity and meanneſs. They are willing to derive benefit from the labours and dangers which they began with decrying, and would eſtabliſh the merit of having foreſeen thoſe diſcoveries which they have gravely pronounced impoſſible.

As to moral cauſes and their effects, they are a perpetual contradiction to the boaſted powers of penetration. The wiſeſt man in general ſees but little before him, and frequently not at all. The objects are ſometimes ſo dark, that it is impoſſible to diſtinguiſh them ; ſometimes ſo luminous, that they dazzle the obſerver's eye ; and paſſion, prejudice, and ſuperſtition, are perpetually buſy to change their colouring and alter their dimenſions. If your lordſhip foreſaw the independence of the Americans, when the Britiſh parliament as wantonly as fooliſhly choſe to drive them to extremities, was every man even of ſenſe endowed with equal penetration?—Many, I believe, as quick-ſighted as yourſelf, and as

much

much the friends of univerfal liberty, trembled for the event. They did not indeed doubt that America would be fevered in the end from the mother country, but they could not fo eafily calculate what might be the immediate effects of the almoft unparalleled forces which this country employed againft it. Neither could they forefee that happy feries of blunders and abfurdity which marked the operations of the Britifh Miniftry, and which contributed, at leaft as much as arms, to bring the affair fo fpeedily to a decifion. They knew they had much to expect from the genius of Lord - - - - -; but they did not exactly comprehend the full extent of his abilities. That wife procraftination of events in their own nature inevitable ; that judicious mixture of precipitance and delay, of firmnefs and pliability ; fo conftantly mifapplied that it is fcarcely poffible to attribute it wholly to the common principles of minifterial dulnefs ; that lethargy that flumbered over every opportunity ; that activity which never failed to fucceed its irremediable lofs ; that plaufibility which never deceived, and that fortitude which never impofed ; were happy ftrokes of the fublime in his lordfhip's character, which required a full feries of feven years to develop to the public.

Pardon me, my lord, a digreffion which the

con-

confideration of fuch unequalled merit draws from my unwilling pen. The noble character which I have been defcribing, has done much for politicians and hiftorians, and he deferves all that they can beftow.

But if the profpect of diftant events is in its own nature fo obfcure as generally to elude or dazzle the ftrongeft fight, is it from the avowed friends of liberty that we are to expect every degree of ridicule and imputation upon thofe who dedicate their lives to its preferva-tion?—The prefent, it is too generally known, is no common or trifling æra. A great and mighty nation, fhaken by fucceffive ftrokes, totters upon its foundations. The nobleft con-ftitution in the world " is fquirted to death by Eton boys." " Parliament, to which it is na-tural to have recourfe in times of difficulty and danger, is, I fear, fallen too much into the public contempt to be of any material fervice. It is, I doubt, too generally looked upon as a body of men without any fixed principles of right and wrong; a weathercock, that obeys each blaft of court or popular favour, which ever of them is uppermoft *." The inevitable conclufion that follows from the premifes laid

---

* Argument to prove, &c. by John, Earl of Stair, p. 33.

down

down by the greateſt calculator in the nation, is, " *That the ſtate is a bankrupt, and that thoſe who have truſted their all to the public faith, are in very imminent danger of becoming (I die pronouncing it) beggars* †." It is true, indeed, your lordſhip adds, if nothing effectual is done to prevent theſe conſequences. But whence is this *ſomething effectual* to ariſe? You have already decried all parties, and have deſcribed the wiſdom and virtue of parliament too exactly to induce us to expect it from that honorable houſe. Nothing, therefore, remains, but the euthanaſia of the conſtitution, towards which you ſeem to caſt a longing eye, the mild deſpotiſm which has eſcaped your pen, that is to indemnify us for all our loſſes, extend the preſent *narrow* bounds of public credit, and prepare us for new wars, with all their baneful attendants.

Were I inclined to imitate your lordſhip's candour, I might pronounce all this, as you do of the wiſhes and exertions of the people, " moſtly impracticable nonſenſe." But I reſpect your lordſhip more than you ſeem to do the ſincereſt friends of their country. In ſuch a ſtate of things, we can no longer be called upon

---

† Argument to prove, &c. p. 32.

to content ourfelves with the common beaten
tracts of political corruption and minifterial cun-
ning. Even the advocates of 'arbitrary power,
fince they have abandoned, their jus divinum
and hereditary right in favour of the houfe of
Hanover, and even your countrymen, fince they
have transferred their attachment from the
name of Stuart to that of Brunfwick, make pro-
tection and obedience infeparable terms. In
the prefent ftate of things, we feem to be almoft
as much abandoned by our governors, as we
formerly were by the Romans, to our own internal ftrength. The land-marks of the conftitution are all removed, and, were we as flavifhly
inclined as the antient Cappadocians, who defired a king becaufe they could not conceive the
poffibility of governing themfelves, we know
not how to obey, becaufe it is not determined
who is to command. Your lordfhip, indeed,
comes forward with a charitable zeal, and offers
us a tyrant. This, perhaps it may be obferved,
is no new prefent from your country ; but almoft a century of civil conteſts and defolations,
of private miferies and public executions,
of controverted titles, and the laſt extremes
alternately dared and fuffered by a noble nation,
have made us rather cautious how we accept
the boon. Let us, in the mean time, try what

can

ean be effected by methods more adapted to the genius and spirit of the English people. No nation was ever deserted by heaven or fortune till it was first deserted by itself; and the annals of our history may lead us to hope that we are never nearer to our deliverance than when a feeble mind sees nothing around but horror and despair.

MARIUS.

LETTER V.

TO THE

Right Honourable the EARL of STAIR.

My LORD,

HE that difinterestedly dedicates his life to the public fervice, if fuch a character can be allowed to exift, is, unlefs virtue be thought its own reward, more to be pitied than every other defcription of men. In the courfe of his labours, he will be obliged fuccefively to attack, if not to join, every party of the great and powerful; and as the malice has always been allowed to exceed the gratitude of our fellow-creatures, he will have much more to expect from the revenge of thofe he quits, than from the patronage of thofe with whom he leagues.

Were a prudent man, therefore, to form a filent and reflected fcheme of making his for-

tune

tune by the public, he would naturally attach
himself to one of the reigning parties into which
this miserable country is divided. It matters
not whether the engagements be formed in the
hour of triumph or disgrace. Success naturally
expands the heart; and defeat has a wonderful
tendency to increase the powers of sensibility.
A routed faction is never squeamishly nice in
admitting friends, or a victorious one in convert-
ing enemies. What wonders have we not already seen performed during the administration
of Lord North! What additional miracles still
attend him in his disgrace!

'There are, my lord, who have imagined you'
composed of such stubborn materials as resist
all the alchymy of modern statesmen. The liberal, the inherited abuse you have so repeatedly
heaped upon ministers and parliaments, seemed
to point you out as one of the few unvitrifiable
substances which no political flux could mollify.
But I have attended, with that prudent jealousy
which ever accompanies a long experience of
mankind, to the progress of your political career. I have discovered, or fancied that I discovered, " a method in your madness ;" a prudence which rarely accompanies violent passions,
but which has never failed to temper the ebul-

litions

litions of your zeal. When in the midst of all your resentment of public wrongs, and even in the more sincere complaint of private injuries, I observed that caution which always distinguished accurately between the sovereign and the minister, I began to think it possible, that all these blunt professions of rugged honesty might mean as little as the tropes and figures of the opposition. Nothing can be more illiberal than national reflections. I admire the industry, the ingenuity, the bravery of your countrymen; but I suspect their patriotism. Rochefaucault observes that the character of every country is as indelibly stamped upon the manners of the individual, as its accent is upon his pronunciation. Will your lordship pretend to constitute the exception?

I anticipate what may be alleged in your defence. It will be observed that duty to the sovereign was never yet reputed treason against the constitution. All the scurrilities which disgrace the press will be produced, from the invectives of the North Briton, down to the pointed malevolence of Junius. But is there no medium between the ruffian and the parasite? Can your lordship conceive no modification of the English language, which does not ter-

terminate either in licentious abuſe, or intereſted flattery?

This nation has been too repeatedly deceived
not to preſerve an active jealouſy. We view
the lion's den, and we are obliged to exclaim
with the fox in the fable, " Veſtigia nulla retror-
" ſum." Not every one that comes to us in
the name of the conſtitution, can be now admitted to the rank and conſequence of a patriot.
It is one of the characteriſtics of the latter
times, that there ſhall ariſe falſe prophets, and
falſe teachers, that ſhall deceive even the elect.
Since, therefore, you have as yet produced no
miracles, nor even pretended to the power of
working them, we muſt try your ſpirit, not by
the marvels you perform, but by the doctrines
you preach.

There is, my lord, a certain ſpecies of pro-
feſſion, a faſhionable cant, which is with juſtice
ſuſpected by every diſcerning mind. It has
been one of the greateſt misfortunes of the
preſent reign, that ſtrong profeſſions of loyalty
and perſonal attachment have always prevailed
over every other ſpecies of political merit. The
obſervation is ſtale, but it is true, that kings are
forbidden by nature to have a friend. Is it their
bleſſing, or their curſe, that they are ſeldom
acquainted

acquainted with this great truth, till it is too late to profit by the difcovery?

The real and difinterefted friend of his country is indeed loyal, but it is loyalty of another ftamp which he profeffes, and which is the principle of his actions. His allegiance to the prince is founded upon the confideration that royalty is an effential part of that conftitution which is the object of all his care and reverence. He confiders not the perfon, but the office of the king. The one is frequently not more refpectable than the meaneft of his fubjects, while the other is immortal and unchangeable. The refpect, therefore, which he bears to the throne will never degenerate into any idolatry for the individual who is feated upon it. If he is ready to defend its juft rights and prerogatives, it is becaufe thofe rights and prerogatives conftitute the Englifh conftitution ; and that conftitution, with all its defects, is more favourable to public happinefs and liberty, than any other which could be adopted. In office, he will treat his fovereign with refpect, and perform his orders with alacrity and zeal ; fo long as thofe orders contribute to the public benefit, and are confiftent with public liberty. He will endeavour to preferve unfullied the nobleft of the royal prerogatives, the power of pro-

G   moting

moting merit and rewarding virtue. Far from
him that abject fpirit of monopolization, which
feizes upon royal favour, as it would do a private patrimony, and proftitutes it to family con-
nections and party leagues. Far from him that
fervile fpirit of flattery, which confounds the
office of minifter and laureate, and degrades
the ruler of a powerful nation into the obfequi-
oufnefs of a court buffoon. He will endeavour
to make the fovereign worthy of the nobleft
panegyrics; but he will teach him to expect
them not from the corrupt echoes of a court,
but from the unbiaffed acclamations of a grateful people:

Alike undaunted amid the tempefts of popular clamour and factious oppofition, he will
keep his eye fixed upon that facred mean which
conftitutes the fecurity of fovereign and people.
Should there be a meafure which his fuperior
genius points out as neceffary to the public
fafety, he will boldly adopt it; defpifing alike
the arts of defigning men, and the empty prejudices of a multitude. He will truft to the
uniform integrity of his own conduct for a vin-
dication; and to time, which as neceffarily
eftablifhes the folid fabrics of truth as it fweeps
away the empty fyftems of falfehood. His fame,
he knows, is not the tranfitory beam of either
royal

royal or popular favour; it is the refult of a
whole feries of confiftent actions directed to one
great end, and proceeding from one common
principle.

That principle may teach him to oppofe the encroachments of faction upon the royal prerogative; but it will teach him to oppofe, with ten-fold
zeal, thofe temporary paroxyfms of delirium which
tempt a deluded people to lay their privileges
at a mafter's feet. In the firft cafe, they may
indeed endanger all, by grafping at too much;
but in the fecond they give up all, even without
the hope of an equivalent. Is the fovereign
virtuous? He will be the laft either to perfuade
or to accept the facrifice. Is he poffeffed with
the common rage of encreafing his power? That
day which yields the conftitution up to his difcretion, renders him a tyrant, and deftroys the
nation.

In what language, therefore, would fuch a
man addrefs the firft magiftrate of his country,
were it neceffary to approach the throne? With
refpect and modefty, but with firmnefs; with
reverence, but with truth. He would leave the
interefted profeffions of perfonal attachment and
veneration to thofe who meant to betray the
people by flattering the fovereign, or to expofe
the fovereign himfelf by foothing the common

prejudices.

prejudices of his ſtation. Should he ſee the nation almoſt undone by a diſaſtrous war, in which a
favourite and protected adminiſtration had borne
a principal ſhare, he would not make his com-
miſeration of injured royalty the capital figure of
the piece. Well knowing that the ſovereign
and his family are always the laſt to feel the
weight of public miſery, he would reſerve his
pi·y for the thouſand innocent objects which deſerve it better. Could he weep tears more faſt
or precious " than the Arabian tree", there would
not be one to beſtow on every victim of ſuch a
war .as the American has produced. If he is
feelingly alive to the temporary embarraſſment of
a *royal hart* held for a moment at bay, what
muſt he feel for whole provinces that have been
for ſeven years the prey of the bloodieſt hunters
that ever followed the chace of death ? What
muſt he feel for a thouſand gallant veterans that
line our ſtreets, deform our public ways, and
preſent in· vain their wounds, their poverty, their
incurable diſeaſes, to thoſe in whoſe pernicious
cauſe they have contracted them ? What muſt
he feel for a nation like the Engliſh, which is,
with all its ·faults, one of the moſt gallant, generous, and deſerving in the·univerſe, reduced
to univerſal beggary by a conteſt which never
was national;: in a diſpute which never intereſted
the public ?

The

The royal children, my lord, have never yet wanted bread *, and Heaven forbid they fhould ever incur that neceffity! They live in the midft of a nation that is fufficiently difpofed to fhare its own laft morfels with its rulers. But perhaps it might be more difcreet in a loyal fubject, to keep the hydra debts of the civil lift, that "bougeon" fo repeatedly, though lopped and feared fo often, and the neceffity of incurring new expences, from the public view. Even Lord A———n's declaration in favour of a *manly and fpirited prince* has met with few admirers. Accuftomed as we are to bear, with a degrading patience, the vices and follies of our rulers, we have not yet learned to believe that they add more to the glory than to the happinefs of the people ; and in our prefent circumftances, we fhould willingly exchange the luftre of fuch a triumph for the more fober advantages of order and œconomy.

MARIUS.

* " The king is forced to take the very bread from his children's mouths." Argument to prove, &c. p. 12.

LET-

LETTER VI.

TO THE

Right Honourable the EARL of SHELBURNE.

My LORD,

IF praife be ever agreeable to a delicate tafte, it is when it afcends pure and unfufpected; fuch an offering as an honeft mind may beftow, and a generous one accept without a blufh. This is what your lordfhip has been little accuftomed to receive during the fhort period of your political triumphs, and what you are too well acquainted with the world to expect during your difgrace. But,

> " When intereft calls off all her fneaking train,
> " And all the oblig'd defert and all the vain :"

then is the hour for the impartial man to come forward, and declare his fentiments. Nor can you be more furprifed at this addrefs, which you certainly have never paid for, than I am, to find a fingle action in a minifter worthy of unbought applaufe. But it appears to me an unpardonable weaknefs to be more afraid of com-

mending

mending merit than of cenfuring vice. I therefore feize the moment, when I find myfelf able
to approve the conduct of a minifter, left it fhould
not return.

When, in the beginning of the year 1782,
we beheld the diffolution of Lord North's adminiftration, you have not forgotten the general
triumphs of the nation. It was not only the
capricious love of novelty, however univerfal
may be the principle; it was the involuntary in-
toxication of a whole people, that, wearied with
its miferies, expected fome relief from a change
of mafters. Befides, the very nature of the circumftances had created in the nation an unufual
difpofition for confidence. The fpirit of oppofition
had raged fo long in vain, that it had drawn the
bonds of political union tighter than common
between the multitude and their leaders. With
whatever contempt the illuftrious characters that
compofe the Houfe of Commons are accuftomed
to treat their conftituents, a variety of caufes had
concurred to produce a temporary relaxation.

The reigning faction could not be ignorant
that it was dangerous to reduce even flaves to
defperation; and a ten years bitter abftinence
from all the fweets of power and emolument had
taught their opponents the neceffity of conde-
fcending to cajole the people. Hence arofe
those

thofe meetings and affociations throughout England ; popular dinners and popular harangues ;
fervent profeffions and unfubftantial promifes;
with all the train of amorous lies and perjuries,
by which our unfuccefsful ftatefmen are accuftomed to enfnare a fond, believing multitude.
And fo thoroughly were they deceived, that they
had entirely forgotten that almoft invariable law
of nature, by which a minifter is compelled to
contradict all that he had ever promifed when
out of place. They perhaps imagined that fomething was to be expected from the unparalleled
extremities to which the whole nation was reduced. They thought that a rational felf-intereft
might for once fupply the place of virtue, and
convince their friends of the utility of preferving
fome appearance of honour and confiftency.
Men that were obtruded againft the confent of
the fovereign might perceive the importance of
cultivating the efteem of the people. There
was too a fort of religious fanctity attached to
the remembrance of common dangers and the
ties which they had produced. The pilfering
Arab, although inured to fpoil and carnage,
will fpare the wretch that has once claimed the
hofpitality of his roof: and who could tell but
Englifh patriots might fo far adopt the example,
as for once to *fpare their friends ?*

But

But there is a fublimity which diftinguifhes
certain minds, although it muft ever efcape
the conceptions of the vulgar. Doomed to the
uniformity of private life, they find it difficult
to conceive what is placed beyond the reach of
common experience. They have indeed a grofs
and confufed fufpicion that the inflexible patriot
may be gradually foftened into the cringing
courtier, or the rapacious minifter; and that
the warmeft advocates for liberty may at length
incline to the folid bleffings of arbitrary power.
But thefe changes they imagine will be the
effect of time and folicitation. They look for
the common formalities of gradual corruption,
and think it hardly poffible that their warmeft
friends fhould become their moft determined
enemies, without paffing through the medium
of neglect and indifference.

But thefe are prejudices which are now happily removed for ever; and I will venture to
affert that the greateft mafter of political verfatility will find it difficult hereafter to attract
applaufe or furprize an audience. Proteus himfelf, were he now to vifit our ifland, muft own
himfelf outdone, even at his own weapons, and
confefs the fuperiority of fome of our modern
practitioners. Although a god, there were
certain ties which could hold him faft, and at

H

length

length compel him to affume his own, after he had run through every other fhape. What would he have faid to mere mortals, who efcape from every tie and put off every character at will?

But, my lord, I am wandering wide of the intended mark. The tafk which I have propofed to myfelf is that of collecting facts, and prefenting fober reafon to my countrymen; and I haften to fulfil it. However eager, however general were the expectations of the people at the change of minifters which took place in the fpring of 1782, they were moft bitterly difappointed. The unfortunate death of the Marquis of Rockingham, which fo fpeedily enfued, was the fignal for breaking up that adminiftration, which twenty years had fcarcely matured, and from which the nation expected its deliverance. I, indeed, had not been one of that fanguine body. Perhaps my dulnefs or malevolence rendered me lefs clear-fighted in refpect to the expected bleffings. My acquaintance with general hiftory, as well as my experience of mankind, had taught me to believe too generally perhaps of public men, that, whatever might be their profeffions, their aim was nothing but felf-intereft. I was not fo partial to the fpirit of the age as to believe it very prolific in fuperior characters.

characters. When I considered the formal professions and the apparent strength and discipline
of our parties, they might appear sufficiently
formidable; but when, after the example of
Agesilaus*, I separated them into their respec-
tive classes, I found the number of genuine
patriots surprizingly diminished. I did not
therefore expect to see the golden days, of
which so many dreamed, renewed or realized,
even under a genuine Whig administration;
which had been the Panacea so industriously
held forth for every national disease. But I
must confess I expected more from the good

---

* When Agesilaus commanded the allied army of the
Grecians in an expedition into Asia, he was reproached for
the small comparative number of Spartans which he had
brought with him. He, therefore, took an opportunity, at
a general review, of proclaiming that all who practised the
trade of carpenters should leave their arms, and go to a
particular spot. Many of the allies, who had been brought
up to that trade, accordingly quitted the ranks, but not a
single Spartan. In this manner he went through every
mechanical trade, till the ranks of the allies were almost
reduced to nothing, while those of the Spartans had suffered
no diminution. " See now," said he, to those who had
before murmured, " on which side the balance preponde-
rates : you bring into the field a numerous band of tradef-
men and mechanics; but it is Sparta alone that furnishes
soldiers."—Probably the author was considering the effect
which would be produced upon a certain honorable house
by a similar proclamation.

sense.

fenfe and abilities of thofe gentlemen than has
been yet performed. I, indeed, forefaw that all
the boafted fchemes of reformation would end
in appropriating the honours and emoluments
of the ftate to themfelves and their creatures ;
but I thought fomething might have been done
for the nation in points where the immediate
intereft of minifters was not concerned. I
imagined the firft object of a fet of men, who
came into power upon the exprefs condition of
reftoring peace, would be to realize the expectations of the public in that particular. I thought
too fomething might be done to heal the wounds
which war had made, and to regain the commercial confidence of the Americans ; not by
facrificing the intereft or honour of the nation,
but by a rational confideration of what its
neceffities required *. In refpect to the additional burthens which every difcerning man
knew muft be impofed, I thought that fome
regard might be fhewn to commerce, to policy,
and even to the inclinations of a people that had
already borne fo much, and with fuch unparalleled patience.

* This fubject has been lately moft fenfibly and forcibly
treated in a pamphlet, by Brian Edwards, Efq.

But,

But, it feems, thefe expectations, moderate as they may appear, were doomed to be difappointed in a manner which it was impoffible to forefee. The premature death of the Marquis of Rockingham broke down the ifthmus which feparated the hoftile factions of the cabinet, and let in the contending tides. I was moft fincerely grieved for that premature death, and lamented it perhaps as truly, though not as indifcreetly, as fome of his friends. I did not indeed attribute any very extenfive range to the political abilities of the noble perfonage, and I always dreaded the fafcinations of party; but he appeared to be a man of amiable and unblemifhed manners, a promoter of agriculture and induftry, and a fincere friend to what he conceived to be the real interefts of his country. Above all, fortune had made him the central point which fupported a mighty arch; an arch indeed more deftined to record the triumphs of a party than the happinefs or liberty of a nation; but fuch an one as could not be then deftroyed, without threatening to involve both in the wide compafs of its ruin.

I know not what were the exact feelings of the nation, when they firft heard of that fatal and irreparable breach in the cabinet, but I will take the liberty of defcribing my own. Whatever

ever credit I might give to the underftandings of the two honorable gentlemen who fet the example of refignation, I did not think that conduct afforded a very favourable fpecimen of either their heads or hearts. I could not conceive that a real friend to any intereft of his country would take that opportunity of wreaking his perfonal fpite, at the expence of the public. Unamimity I had heard echoed, at every public meeting, by every fubaltern of the party, till I was fickened with the found. Was it then a time, in fuch an awful moment of national crifis and danger, to perplex the public councils with the low interefts and cabals of faction, at the expence of that very unanimity which had till then been the *word* of the whole party? The public at large can fcarcely pretend to decide the paltry quarrels of courts and cabinets; but they felt, that if there was ever an hour when an honeft man would have conceded fomething for the general good, it was the prefent; and they cared not who was prime minifter, provided he gave them peace.

I am almoft afraid your lordfhip will hardly excufe the ftyle of even this panegyric: if you do not, I can eafily conceive in what manner it will be received by others. But this is the language of truth; and thefe are the fenti-

ments

ments of every independent man throughout
the kingdom with whom I have converfed.

But when the feffion was opened with that
memorable fpeech which has been fo much
the fubject of altercation, I could not help feel-
ing fomething like furprize at the manner in
which it was received. Had the lower houfe
been peopled indeed with inveterate republicans,
I fhould have been lefs furprized at the
fpirit which guided thofe memorable debates:
but when I faw thofe very gentlemen, who
had fo lately given fpecimens of their extraordinary talents for abject flattery, dealing
out the moft unmannerly invectives, I could
not help blufhing for human nature and my
country.

In fpite, however, of virulence, fcurrility, and
oppofition, the peace was ratified by the fame
honorable gentlemen whofe confciences would
not fuffer them to approve it. Common minds,
indeed, did not comprehend the full force of
thofe fubtle diftinctions. They thought that
if the peace was pernicious and difhonorable,
it merited the public oppofition of the houfe.
They thought it as much an object of parliamentary interference, as the nomination of
a new minifter, the firft, and moft undoubted
prerogative of the crown. The nomination of

an

an improper minifter may be indeed eventually deftructive to a nation ; but it is not a meafure which requires fuch immediate interference. A virtuous and independent houfe of commons, like the prefent, may always arreft him in his career ; they always poffefs the dreadful artillery of impeachments, of which they have made fo liberal an ufe during this whole century ; they may at any time fend forth their thunders, and hurl him flaming down. But an inadequate and difhonorable peace may reduce the nation, in an inftant, to fuch extremities, as may render all future exertions vain.

But the peace was to be reprobated in order to difplace the minifter. There was even a peculiar advantage in making him the facrifice of the only falutary meafure which this country has feen during the laft twenty years. Even in the hour of triumph and exultation, no peace which is upon record has ever fatisfied the ex-pectations of the nation. How then was it poffible that a peace, which was to ratify the eternal divorce of America, and which muft therefore be attended with fome humiliation to this country, could pleafe the wild imagi-nations of the people ; a people who had fuffered enough to ficken them with war, but not enough to make them fubmit with
equanimity

equanimity to the difadvantages of their fituation ? It is the peculiar mifery of human beings
never to forefee inconveniences while they may
be avoided, or to be able to bear them with
patience when they are inevitable.

That the peace was the beft which might have
been obtained, it is impoffible for me to decide.
That it included the beft terms your lordfhip
was able to procure, may be fufficiently inferred,
even from the principles of ambition and felf-
love : that any of your rivals would have been
able to make a better, we have never had a
more convincing proof than their own affertions.
Such therefore as it is, the merit of it is entirely
your own.

Whoever is moderately acquainted with human affairs, will continually lament the blindnefs both of princes and ftates. An ufelefs
tract of defert, a frozen ocean, a barren rock,
may each in turn become the object of jealoufy
and ambition ; may deluge the earth with blood,
or cover the fea with carnage. But the folid
advantages of peaceful induftry, the perfection
of internal government, and the improvement of
agriculture, are objects that are either overlook-
ed, or rarely fuffered to incline the fcale. Yet
it would not be difficult to prove that there
never has exifted a nation, which would not

I   have

have been more benefited by applying its attention to these constant sources of happiness and population, than by a series of the most splendid conquests. Yet war is sometimes inevitable; a frantic prince, an ambitious minister, even a favoured parasite, or strumpet, may each alternately endanger the freedom and existence of all the neighbouring states. Every nation must therefore be prepared to defend by arms those rights which may be attacked by arms; and when the contest is once begun, the soundest policy consists in the most vigorous efforts. But when the dispute does not relate either to national safety or independence, but to points of ideal power and speculative ambition; to something which flatters the pride more than it concerns the interest of a nation; above all, when it has originated in the spirit of error, and been carried on by that of delusion, it cannot too soon receive its termination.

That this was the case with the American war, it would now be loss of time to attempt to prove. As to the object of that contest, the minister that brought it on was continually shifting his ground; but, whatever was the pretext, it always implied the subjection of the colonies. When this too, like all the rest, had deserted him; when that subjection had been given up

by

by every party as impracticable, the spirit of infatuation itself could scarcely invent a reason
for continuing the war, the instant a tolerable
peace was attainable. If there has been a set
of men in this country sufficiently blind, and
adverse to their country's interests, to attempt
to continue it, your lordship will never blush
to reckon them in the number of your enemies.

As to most of the reasons which I have heard
alleged, they disgrace even the logic of the
house of commons. So very contemptible and
scanty were they, that even the unhappy loyalists
have been dragged into the question, by the very
persons that had so frequently represented them
as the vile incendiaries of the war. That the situation of many of these unhappy men is truly
pitiable I do not deny; that they deserve well
of the government, whatever they may do of
the nation, is equally certain : but that it was
necessary to carry on the war upon their account
alone, I think the spirit of party itself will
hardly venture to assert. If it was impracticable
to conquer America for the British sovereign,
or the British parliament, did it cease to be so,
when attempted in the name of the loyalists?
Or will any one dare to assert that any thing,
short of conquest, could have forced the Americans to admit them to what they had lost. If

there-

therefore they wifhed to be reftored to their native country, it was evident that a fingle year
of peace would operate more in their favour,
by abating the animofity of their countrymen,
than could have been effected by half a century
of arms. If they only defired a compenfation
for their loffes, the faving of a dozen or twenty
millions in the national expenditure, would
nearly have paid the bill, though it had been
indorfed by all their friends in the oppofition.

But what fhall we reply to the heavier charges
of national difgrace, incurred by the ceffion of
a barren wafte, or a narrow ifland, to our enemies? Simply this, that public honour will always be better preferved by augmenting the
power, than by adding to the weaknefs of a
nation. The relative ftrength of every nation
can never be long a fecret to its neighbours;
and the opinion which they entertain of this
particular, will always be the meafure of the
refpect which they fhew, not the detail of paft
achievements, or the vain remembrance of a
prowefs it can no longer boaft. If this principle be true, it is evident, that great Britain,
if doomed to lofe the colonies, became actually
more formidable the inftant a peace had taken
place, than fhe had been at any moment fince
the confederacy of fo many nations againft her.

The

The power of every ſtate is merely relative, and muſt be eſtimated not by any univerſal ſtandard, but by the comparative force of its neighbours. It is evident that during all the latter years of the war, however great might be the efforts of this country in themſelves, they were inadequate to the object propoſed: they were inadequate to the conqueſt of America; they were even inadequate to the defence of all our own poſſeſſions. But why were they inadequate? Merely for the ſame reaſon that Horatius was inferior to the united force of his three enemies, though ſingly more than a match for either. A confederacy had been formed againſt this country, ſuch as we have no precedent of in the annals of our hiſtory; ſuch as it will be our own fault, if we are doomed to encounter a ſecond time. Would it not have been reputed a maſter-ſtroke of policy to have been able to detach a ſingle member of that confederacy from the reſt, and to have decreaſed the ſuperiority of our enemies? Mr. Fox is ſaid to have tried the experiment with Holland, and your lordſhip with America: we have great reaſon to be thankful that both the attempts were abortive.

But, in giving us peace, you effected infinitely more than it was poſſible to do by any other means.

You

You broke to pieces, at a ftroke, that vaft co-
loffus of a league which threatened to crufh us
with its weight, and fcattered the fragments abroad
to all the winds. You gave us time to repair the
ruined ftate of our finances by the admirable bills
of reform which Mr. Burke has introduced ; and
to regain the friendfhip of America by the falutary
proclamations of laft July. And if the affairs of
India had been as wifely and equitably fettled as
they were intended by Mr. Fox's bill, fome part
of the glory muft have been due to you, who
prepared the way, by removing every obftruction.

Where then is the lofs of national honour? If
national honour confift in fuch a mafs of force as
is fingly fuperior to all that can be brought againft
it, fuch national honour never has yet exifted.
It did not exift even in the proudeft times of the
Roman commonwealth ; fince no one can doubt
that the art of dividing enemies and poftponing
wars contributed, no lefs than arms, to the eftablifhment of their greatnefs. To look for it in the
nicely-balanced fyftem of contrary forces which
now compofe the ftate of Europe, would be the
extreme of folly ; fince the very ftability of that
ftate is confeffedly owing to the power of oppofing
the ambition of one nation by the union of all the
reft. Why then fhould the Englifh people defire
impoffibilities,

impoffibilities, which, even could they be realized, would end in their own deftruction; fince
every human power, which becomes too mighty
for refiftance, muft neceffarily produce every fpecies of internal diforder and corruption?

But whether they perfift in the purfuit of this
chimerical greatnefs, or bound their wifhes with
the folid enjoyment of national happinefs and fecurity, it is demonftrable that peace was neceffary
for either object. A war, in which we were fo
evidently overmatched, and the continuance of
which exhaufted our national refources fo faft,
without any adequate means of fupply, could
never have given us that decided fuperiority which
the fucceffes of Lord Chatham himfelf had failed
to do. Peace therefore became neceffary, were
it only in the view of promoting the objects of
our own ambition.

But the honour of a nation is not to be rated
by the chimerical ftandard of its being fingly
able to ftand againft the world in arms, or by a
ruinous obftinacy in purfuing impracticable projects. It is to be rated by the opinion of its wifdom and juftice, joined with fuch a degree of
power as renders it fecure from every probable attack: and all thefe objects were more attainable
by peace, than by the bloodieft continuance of
the

the war. Our wifdom can never be impeached
by putting an end to a ruinous conteft which had
no longer an object; our juftice, by defifting from
injuring the Americans and the Dutch; or our
power, by ceafing to lavifh our blood and treafures
as unprofitably as we had hitherto done.

And if we poffeffed fufficient power to carry on
the war for feveral future years, will any of thofe
refources be diminifhed by the peace? Will they
not, on the contrary, be continually increafing, unlefs our late infatuation is doomed to attend us to
the laft? By the equity and moderation of our
public counfels we certainly may prevent the poffibility of fuch a league as we have lately efcaped:
and which of our neighbours will *fingly* chufe to
encounter a nation that has been fo nearly equal
to all combined?

Thefe, my lord, are the reflections of an impartial man upon the peace which you have given
us. In every point of view it rifes upon the underftanding, and is brought home to our convic-
tion. If the arguments I have ufed be juft, they
may tend to diminifh the remaining prejudices of
our countrymen, and to refcue one action of a
minifter from the general infamy which awaits
the tribe. If they be, on the contrary, falfe, and
liable to be refuted, the malice of your enemies

is

is not fo much affuaged, as to allow them any
permanent triumphs. And while your lordfhip
will efcape the ridicule of employing fo weak an
advocate, I fhall defervedly engrofs the whole difgrace of the undertaking, who,

"Nec Dîs, nec viribus, æquis,"

have engaged a volunteer in fuch a caufe.

MARIUS.

LETTER VII.

To Edmund Burke, Esq.

SIR,

IT is not without a diffidence proportioned to your great abilities and fame, that in the courſe of my labours I addreſs myſelf to you.

> , . . . But if I muſt contend,
> Beſt with the beſt . . . more glory will be won,
> Or leſs be loſt.—

And there is a paſſage in your own ſpeech of the firſt of December laſt which emboldens me to the attempt, and makes me triumph over the conſideration of my own inferiority. You ob-ferve, ſir, " that nothing is to be found in any habits of life or education, which tends wholly to diſqualify men for the functions of govern-ment, but that by which the power of exer-ciſing thoſe functions is very frequently obtained ; I mean a ſpirit of low cabal and intrigue, which I have never, in one inſtance, ſeen united

with

with a capacity for found and manly policy*." If
this, fir, is any criterion, I can appeal to my own
heart, and folemnly declare that I am as little connected with any cabal or intrigue, as any one in
your own virtuous and independent majority; as
little as yourfelf, Lord North, and Mr. Fox.

But before I begin to ftate the obfervations
with which I intend to trouble you, I will take
the liberty of fettling the limits within which
our controverfy will be confined. I do not
mean to expatiate in the wide field of accufations
which are brought againft the Eaft-India company : I cannot pretend to be prepared by " three
years of laborious parliamentary refearch," or
armed with the artillery of fecret committees ;
whofe reports are now the unerring dictates of
truth, though in the year 1781 they were " the
curfed Pandora's box, whence fprung- out that
dreadful calamity, the American war." Thefe
laurels, fir, are all your own; they have been
dearly earned, and it would be equal temerity and
injuftice to difturb you in their poffeffion. My
labours will be of an humbler nature : they
will be confined to thofe points in which every
citizen may with propriety pretend to form a
judgment, the conduct of our reprefentatives,

* Mr. Burke's Speech on the firft of December, 1783,
p. 11, printed for Dodfley.

K 2

in meddling with the affairs of the Eaſt-India company; the virtue of the attempt, and the wiſdom of their proceedings.

A perſon ſo intimately acquainted with human life and literature, as I confeſs you to be, cannot be ignorant that it is one common art of every accuſer to excite the indignation of his audience, by every method within his power. When once their paſſions are thoroughly raiſed by a recital, whether real or fictitious, of crimes and horrors, it becomes eaſy to give the ſtorm whatever direction he wiſhes. Inſtead of being upon our guard againſt the ſuggeſtions of our heated imaginations, inſtead of ſcrutinizing the pretended evidence with a degree of doubt and accuracy proportioned to the enormity of the caſe, we are too apt to accept of violence and exaggeration inſtead of proof. Our very prejudices and indolence, in this caſe, aſſume the form and dignity of virtue; and at length the ſober dictates of caution and impartiality are utterly diſcarded, or treated as enemies, that would ſeduce us from our duty.

It is no wonder, ſir, if this ſhould be particularly true of the noble audience that liſtened to your Philippic. Men of ſuch ſevere and unblemiſhed manners could ſcarcely be expected to preſerve a due and neceſſary moderation at ſuch a

tale

tale of complicated horrors. Whatever could
add either pathos or energy to the description was
certainly introduced. Here was the great Mogul—
" the descendant of Tamerlane, a personage as
high as human veneration can look at," unless
perhaps it be the godlike mover of the bill, "stand-
ing in need almost of the common neceffaries of
life*." Here was Seraja Dowla fold to Mir Jaffeir,
Mir Jaffeir to Mir Coffim; and Mir Coffim to
Mir Jaffeir again †. Then to fhew that the rage
and cruelty of the Eaft-India company's fervants
know no exceptions of fex, or no fex, we are told
a moving hiftory of outrages offered to ladies,

* " The firft potentate fold by the company for money
was the great Mogul—the defcendant of Tamerlane. This
high perfonage, as high as human veneration can look at,"
&c.—Speech, p. 17.

- " The defcendant of Tamerlane now ftands in need almoft of the common neceffaries of life."—Ibid. p. 18.

This fact is moft fatisfactorily explained in many of the
publications in anfwer to Mr. Burke, particularly in the
writings of Major Scott. But what does it add to the atrocity
of the action, that the great Mogul is the defcendant of
Tamerlane? Tamerlane himfelf was a robber and a fpoiler,
and more deftructive to mankind than peftilence, famine, or
even the Eaft-India company.

† Speech, p. 19.

and

and even to eunuchs ‡. The ſtory itſelf of Urſula
and her eleven thouſand virgins is almoſt parallel-
ed in that of the nabob of Oude, his two thouſand
women, the two ſeraglios more of his near kin-
dred, and the nabob's fourſcore children §.

" Quis talia fando
" Temperet a lachrymis ?"

It is true, ſir, that you had like to have ſpoiled
all again by the mention of the venerable " grand-
mother and the ancient houſehold :" this circum-
ſtance was too powerful for the muſcles of the
younger members. But even the great Scriblerus
ſometimes touched the improper ſtring ; and when
you ſum up all, by complimenting the houſe upon
their virtue and independency, it was as impoſſible
they ſhould reſiſt, as an ugly woman who hears
for the firſt time commendations upon her beauty.

‡ " Their chief eunuchs, who were their agents, their
guardians, protectors, perſons of high rank according to the
eaſtern manners, and of great truſt, were thrown into dun-
geons, to make them diſcover their hidden treaſures; and
there they lie at preſent."—Speech, p. 44.

§ " That family and houſehold conſiſted of *two thouſand
women*, to which were added two other ſeraglios of near kin-
dred, and ſaid to be extremely numerous, and (as I am well
informed) of about fourſcore of the Nabob's children, with
all the eunuchs, the ancient ſervants, and a multitude of the
dependants of his ſplendid court."—Ibid, p. 45.

But

But I agree with you, fir, that the prefent is no feafon for mirth or levity ; and I never held the opinion that ridicule was the teft of truth. The points on which we differ are neither to be fettled by raillery nor declamation, but by the fober force of truth and argument ; and to thefe I return.

You obferve, fir, "that the phrafe of the chartered rights of men" is full of affectation, and very unufual in the difcuffion of privileges conferred by charters of the prefent defcription." I have always confidered the expreffion in the fame light, but for another reafon. A charter, if I rightly underftand the expreffion, comprehends certain powers conferred by the king in virtue of his prerogative. The Eaft-India company, I believe, may pretend to this fecurity ; but I fhould hardly think its advocates would much infift upon them, when they can appeal to authorities of higher importance. The firft eftablifhment of the Eaft-India company upon its prefent bafis, was, as you very well know, an act of the whole legiflature in 9th and 10th of William and Mary, which engaged to incorporate the lenders of two millions to the government into a company, and invefted them with certain exclufive rights. So far were the people of that time from infifting upon their chartered rights, that the parliament denied the

power

power of the crown to grant a charter of that defcription ; and the old Eaft-India company exerted all its influence in vain to procure a parliamentary eftablifhment.   And fo great was the difference of ideas which then prevailed, that though
the old Eaft-India company could claim no other
foundation than a royal charter, which had been
repeatedly declared infufficient by the commons,
though it was contended that its members had
been guilty of acts fubverfive of all the rights
which they pretended to, when they were heard
in oppofition before the lords, yet they were quiet-
ly allowed to continue their franchifes, till they
wifely *coalefced* with the new company in 1702,
and put an end to their own feparate exiftence.

The form of that act in 1698, from which the
prefent company derives its eftablifhment, has been
the model of all the fubfequent ones which the
legiflature has chofen to pafs. But the only claufe,
which it is now material to take notice of, is that
which empowers the government, upon re-payment
of the two millions originally borrowed, and giving three years notice after the twentieth of Sep-
tember 1711, to diffolve the faid company, and re-
affume all the powers with which it had been invefted.

Let me now, fir, be permitted to ftop for a
moment, and confider the nature of the tranfaction

action which I have juft defcribed, and which I
believe you will find faithfully copied from the
hiftory of thofe times. Here, then, is a folemn
contract entered into by the whole legiflature on
the one fide, and certain individuals on the other,
which, in confideration of two millions to be advanced for the public fervice, fettles upon them
for a limited time certain exclufive privileges,
with an equity of redemption in cafe it fhould appear inexpedient to continue thofe powers beyond
the appointed period. Can it be fuppofed, therefore, that either of thefe contracting parties was
imagined to retain the right of diffolving the agreement, whenever it fhould judge proper, for rea-
fons of which it was to remain the fole and unac-
countable judge? Is it not, on the contrary, one of
the moft abfurd, ridiculous, and unfounded ideas
that ever entered into the head of a human being,
even into the head of a politician? Where contracts are entered into between one individual and
another, there is always fome public tribunal
which will oppofe injuftice and enforce their obfervance: and I believe, till the celebrated re-
ceipt-tax of laft year, there is fcarcely to be found
an inftance of a government, which did not at
leaft infift upon good faith in its fubjects, whatever indulgences it might allow itfelf.

It is true, fir, that there is one effential dif-

L   ference

ference between a government and an individual :
an individual may be compelled to the obfervance
of his contract, which cannot be done to the
former, unlefs by a general infurrection of the
people and a revolution. But does this make
any difference in refpect to moral obligations or
principles of juftice ? Or is a ftate allowed to
act upon thofe principles, which would indelibly
involve every individual in fuch a web of infamy
and difgrace, as would deftroy his character for
ever ? It may, perhaps, be anfwered, that this
is a liberty in which moft governments have oc-
cafionally indulged themfelves. I grant the fact,
and you will perhaps grant the confequences :
that moft governments have become fo univer-
fally infamous by the practice, that it is difficult
to decide whether they are confidered with more
abhorrence by foreign nations, or by their own
fubjects. I have little occafion to infift upon fome
celebrated manœuvres of this kind in our neighbours ; fince there is fcarcely a gentleman who
voted for the Eaft-India bill, provided he had
words enough to make a motion, that has not,
in fome preceding debate, infifted upon the
immenfe refources of this country in comparifon
with France, all derived from the confiftency of
its conduct, and the vaft extent of its credit.

I muft confefs, fir, I have a kind of antiquated
prejudice

prejudice in favour of confiftency. I can refpeſt men of every different political opinion, provided they are uniform : but I have never been able to underſtand that eternal verfatility of charaſter which changes public debates into the venal eloquence of wrangling lawyers ; nor can I conceive, by any theory which I think myfelf allowed to mention, whence it arifes that thefe fudden flaſhes of new conviſtion are always found to accompany the immediate interefts of the party. The gen-tlemen, who are known by the general name of the Rockingham party, have always diftinguiſhed themfelves by their inveterate oppofition to every parliamentary reform. According to them, it is infinitely better to fuffer the nobleft conftitution of the world to fall into ruins before our eyes, than to change a fingle ftone in the crumbling edifice, or even to add a prop to fupport it. I have liftened, fir, without conviſtion, to much reafoning of this kind ; and, though I do not recolleſt that many gentlemen have chofen to put their names to their elaborate defence of the prefent fyftem, I have always allowed that they might poffibly be in earneft. Were it neceffary, I could produce many inftances of the infinite contempt they heap upon fpeculative principles of right and wrong, and vifionary fyftems of reformation, from all the celebrated pamphlets of the party.

Bu,

But, in the name of God, why do they not ad-
here to their own principles? Are the repeated
agreements which the whole legiflature has made
with the Eaft-India company of lefs fanctity than
the feptennial bill, which even the boldeft of
your own houfe has never yet contended to be
conftitutional; and which not one of you can
now defend, without afferting that you have a
right to fubvert the whole fyftem of government
at your pleafure? Or, is it imagined, that the
folid opinions of mankind upon the fubject of
right and juftice are to be changed by every
temporary blaft that turns the ftate weathercock
of your honorable houfe?

But as to the original act of eftablifhment for
the Eaft-India company, it was penned with all
the requifite difcretion and forefight. It was a
new experiment made upon a very important fubject of political economy, and therefore the
government wifely referved to itfelf a power of
diffolving the company, in cafe experience fhould
evince the neceffity of doing it. But, if they
have never taken advantage of that reftraining
claufe, during the term of almoft an hundred
years, what are we to infer from this forbearance,
excepting that the government found nothing in
this company " worthy of death." For my part,
I attach fo much refpect to the honorable houfe
of

of commons, that I cannot eafily believe it capable of the groffeft contradiction and abfurdity. Now, in my humble opinion, it is difficult to admit this new neceffity of feizing all the property of the Eaft-India company, and fubverting an agreement of the whole legiflature, without throwing fuch infinuations either upon the wifdom or juftice of our reprefentatives, as even their moft inveterate enemy would fcarcely venture.

The laft agreement, fir, which is upon record of the government with the Eaft-India company dates no farther back than the fpring or fummer of the year 1781. Lord North had taken advantage of the approaching expiration of their privilege, to give the requifite notice that he intended to diffolve the company. Had he actually done this, we might have objected to the policy or wifdom of the meafure ; but certainly no one could confiftently have denied the right. But this was by no means done, or perhaps ever intended ; and therefore, after a variety of political altercation, an act paffed in the fame form with all the preceding, to extend the Company's exclufive privileges to the year 1791, in confequence of four hundred thoufand pounds paid to the government.

It is here worth remarking, that the majority, which ratified this agreement, was a majority of

the'

the fame houfe of commons which now exifts ;
and, confequently, I am reduced to the unfortunate dilemma of either believing that the
honorable houfe acquitted the company of all
their crimes and delinquencies to the moment
when the act paffed, or of fuppofing that fo
wife, fo virtuous, fo independent an houfe could
not be ignorant of fuch a baneful catalogue of
crimes, and therefore gravely intended to bite
the nation, and fwindle the company out of
four hundred thoufand pounds, upon a pre-
tence which they never intended to realize.

I have heard it obferved, that a fkilful fencer
never expofes himfelf for the chance of hitting
his adverfary ; yet this feems to be the cafe of
your moft eloquent detail of the pretended
crimes of the company. The greater part of
thefe atrocious acts were certainly prior to the
year 1781. With what propriety, therefore,
with what appearance of juftice does the fame
houfe of commons found a neceffity of refcind-
ing its own deliberate engagements, upon al-
legations, which it either was, or ought to have
been acquainted with, at the very moment when
it contracted them ?

With all the refpect, fir, which we may feel
either for you or your audience, how is it poffible
that any human being fhould avoid fmiling, when

he

he hears the privileges of the company attacked upon the principle of their eſtabliſhing a monopoly, within the walls of that very houſe, which inſtituted the monopoly in the laſt century, and has maintained it by ſucceſſive ſales and contracts throughout the preſent*? Still more

---

* " The Eaſt-India charter is a charter to eſtabliſh monopoly, and to _create_ power. Political power and commercial monopoly are not the rights of men; and the rights to them derived from charters, it is fallacious and ſophiſtical to call " the chartered rights of men." Theſe chartered rights (to ſpeak of ſuch charters and of their effects in terms of the greateſt poſſible moderation) do at leaſt ſuſpend the natural rights of mankind at large, and in their very frame and conſtitution are liable to fall into a direct violation of them."—Speech, p. 7.

All this flouriſh appears to me one of the ſtrongeſt inſtances how a good underſtanding may be abuſed. If a legiſlature attempt to ſell more than it poſſeſſes a right to do, the people may be juſtified, perhaps, in reſcinding an agreement made without their conſent, and to their detriment. But what has all this to do with the legiſlature itſelf, whoſe deciſions are to be law and juſtice for all the reſt of the community, reſcinding its own agreements?—Would not this be a plain confeſſion of ignorance, folly, or injuſtice, in the very perſons who aſſume to themſelves the power of deciding for all the reſt? And if this be found to-day, why not to-morrow? If in the laſt agreement, why not in the next?—Would not this bring the legiſlature into ſuch extreme contempt as would tend either to tyranny, or to a diſſolution of all government?—And is this the noble and excellent ſpirit of reform which is to be introduced into the Engliſh government?— " Unde nefas tantum Latiis paſtoribus?"—

Let

more curious is the diftinction between the ideas of natural and artificial right. What is it to the buyer, whether the houfe choofe to fell one or the other? He naturally expects to be maintained in what he has fairly purchafed. Muft no one pretend to enter into a contract with any government, without the interference of Grotius, Puffendorf, and Montefquieu? Or whence do the honorable gentlemen derive their notions of natural right, when they deny to feven millions of people the leaft interference with the choice of their own reprefentatives?

But what, I wonder, would be faid to any man in private life, who, after having voluntarily and deliberately entered into a contract, fhould pretend to refcind it at will, becaufe it was contrary to his ideas of natural right? Would it not be anfwered, that this was the fillieft pretext by which fraud ever attempted to impofe upon credulity? He would be told that he had fufficient leifure to confider the fubject, and confult the delicay of his feelings, before he entered

Let me be pardoned, if I publicly affert, that fuch an idea is difgraceful to the hitherto untainted reputation of our public faith, and fatal to the confidence which all fubjects ought to entertain in the juftice of the legiflature; worthy only of the fpirit of tyranny, and moft happily adapted to root out honefty and commerce throughout the kingdom.

into

into the engagement: but that little credit would be given to his pretended qualms, when they were evidently dictated by his own interest; that juftice and right were never inconfiftent with themfelves; and that the firft duty of both was to fulfil promifes and engagements.—But what, if all thefe fcruples fhould neither tend to a reftitution of the rights in queftion to thofe from whom they were originally taken, or to any indemnification of their value? Muft we not admire the particular delicacy which breaks its own moft folemn faith and contract, from the fuggeftions of confcience, and then finifhes by violating thofe very rights a fecond time, with as little remorfe as it did the firft?

For to what, fir, do all thefe declamations about right and monopoly tend? Will the natural rights of every fubject in thefe kingdoms to carry on a commerce with India, be lefs invaded when the monopoly is given to feven commiffioners of the parliament, than while it remained in the directors of the company? Or is there the leaft alteration made, or pretended to be made, in the actual ftate of that monopoly?

But the plea of ftate-neceffity, upon which your honorable friend expatiated with fo much eloquence, is a topic much more difficult to be

M   con-

confuted, becaufe it is fo vague and general as
fcarcely to admit an anfwer. Were there fome
inter-mediate power, indeed, to decide between
the contracting parties, it might mean fomething; but in the prefent cafe it means no more
than that a minifter and a majority may, under
the fubterfuge of general and equivocal terms,
violate every engagement they had entered into.
For what enterprife can be conceived fo openly
flagitious and unjuft, which may not be jufti-
fied by the fame perfons, and upon the fame
principles? I will engage to produce an act for
vefting all the looms of Manchefter, or the
forges of Birmingham, in feven commiffioners,
upon the very fame principles of ftate-neceffity
which make fo great a figure in his fpeech.

A great metaphyfician, like you, fir, need
not be told, that the expreffions of right,
juftice, charter, contract, neceffity, and an
hundred more which might be produced, can
never in themfelves decide a fingle controverfy
between two individuals of the human fpecies.
All parties allow their exiftence, and appeal to
them in their own favour. Naturally, the underftanding of one man has an equal claim with
that of any other, to be attended to in the controverfy. But as it is evident, that fcarcely any
difpute would ever be terminated were it to
                                        depend

depend upon the entire acquiefcence of one
party in the reafon of another, public tribunals
are inftituted in every ftate, for the adminiftration of juftice and the termination of differences.
In thefe tribunals, certain individuals are invefted with the power of deciding what fhall be
juftice and law in refpect to the reft of the
fociety ; not from the fuppofition that one man
is naturally more infallible than another, but
becaufe this method, however imperfect, is all
that can be effected by human prudence. It is
poffible to afcertain the perfon, though not the
thing ; and while there are eternal difputes about
law and equity, there is feldom any concerning
the perfon of the judge or chancellor.

To preferve thefe venerable perfonages even
from the fufpicion of corruption ; to guard
againft the furprifes of private prejudice or
paffion ; and to divide the different powers in
fuch a manner as mutually to be a check upon
each other, has long been the diftinguifhing
boaft of our country and conftitution. The
meaneft individual cannot be condemned, without his paffing before fo many independent
authorities as to leave fcarcely a fuppofition of
collufion or injuftice. Firft, he muft be accufed
upon oath before a magiftrate, who ought to
be a private gentleman of independent fortune.

In

In the next place, he muſt be referred to a
body of independent gentlemen, who, if they
judge the accuſation falſe or groundleſs, have a
right of inſtantly diſmiſſing it; and theſe too
are ſworn to the obſervance of impartial juſtice.
In the third place, another jury is inveſted with
the power of finally deciding, upon oath, his
guilt or innocence; and though the number of
this body is only twelve, the criminal may
peremptorily except to twenty of thoſe who are
returned for the office. Theſe men are ex-
preſsly to be choſen out of the peers or equals
of the accuſed; that ſo far from having any
intereſt in his condemnation, they may have the
ſtrongeſt motive to give its proper weight to
every plea which can be brought in his favour.
The indictment too muſt be preciſe and accu-
rate; that no room may be left for the faſcina-
tions of eloquence, or the wild ſuggeſtions of
general and vague accuſation; which are ſeldom
employed but to perplex the mind and bewilder
the judgment.

Theſe, ſir, are the ſecurities which the Engliſh
law affords to the perſon of the meaneſt individual in the kingdom, previous to his being ſub-
jected even to the judicial authority: and I have
mentioned them thus at length, that the public
may contraſt them with the proceedings of a certain

tain honorable houſe in reſpect to the greateſt
company of merchants in the univerſe; men, who,
in whatever light they may be conſidered by mo-
raliſts, have done much for the opulence and
glory of the kingdom. And I muſt confeſs, it
ſtrikes me with no little idea of "the inconſtancy
of human greatneſs, and the ſtupendous revolutions that have happened in our age of wonders,"
when I ſee a ſet of men, who have juſt loſt thir-
teen provinces, ſitting in judgment upon, and
diſpoſſeſſing thoſe who have added to the Britiſh
empire "281,412 ſquare miles; which form a
territory larger than any European dominion,
Ruſſia and Turkey excepted *."

"Nunc et oves ultro fugiat lupus: aurea duræ
"Mala ferant quercus: narciſſo floreat alnus."

Their proceedings have been worthy of the
cauſe; for, in the confuſion of powers and characters which they have aſſumed to themſelves,
it is difficult to diſtinguiſh any thing of reaſon,
juſtice, or even of a regular ſyſtematic enquiry.
Firſt, they chew the cud of evidence and fact in
their ſecret and ſelect committees; which is afterwards to be brought up again half-digeſted, and
to become the loathſome nutriment of a criminal
proſecution. Then, in their judicial character,
they ſit to determine upon the merits of this very

* Speech, p. 12.

evidence,

evidence, which they have before prepared. The accusers are certain orators of their own body; who, instead of confining themselves to specific charges, or any of the salutary forms which long experience has established as neceffary to the impartial administration of juftice, deal out their general invectives, and unfupported accusations, without examining a witnefs, or even waiting for an anfwer. Thus is the affair hurried on according to the true principles of fummary juftice, and brought to a fpeedy termination; and then too, the fame honorable houfe affumes its laft, and, as its enemies would obferve, its moft confiftent character, that of public executioner; difpatches the offender in an inftant, and feizes upon all his fpoils as hangman's wages.

Thus, fir, have I gone through the firft part of my difagreeable tafk, in refpect to the celebrated Eaft-India bufinefs. One plea, indeed, has been omitted, that of an honorable lord, your late enemy, but prefent friend and colleague, who juftifies the invafion of the company's rights by the precedent of his having already violated them in 1772. The argument, I truft, will make but few profelytes out of his own houfe; but it is fuch an illuftration of my fubject that I cannot pafs it over in filence.

To the Englifh nation, therefore, at large I muft

muft recommend the confideration of another
fpecies of neceffity ; the neceffity of watching,
with a fevere and conftant attention, the operations of men who call themfelves the reprefentatives of the people, yet are continually fetting
that people at defiance. They refift, with an inflexible obftinacy, every attempt to bring them
nearer to the only purpofe for which they exift ;
yet there is nothing fo remote, or facred, as to
efcape the interference of their avarice and ambition. Even the moft fcandalous outrages, the
moft unjuftifiable attempts upon the rights of
others, if once fubmitted to, are boldly brought
forward as precedents, and ufed as arguments for
new ones. If a minifter dare fomething of peculiar atrocity or injuftice, " brevibus gyaris aut
carcere dignum," it is railed at by his opponents,
but enforced by a majority of his creatures.
Suppofing the wheel of fortune to turn round,
and the friends of the people to grafp the diftinctions which they long have aimed at, what
is to be expected from their promifes and their
public fpirit ? That they fhould refign the ufurpations of their predeceflors, or endeavour to give
the nation any fecurity for their liberties ? That
indeed would fhew a moft contemptible ignorance
of public men, and the hiftory of parties in this
country. But what you may fafely expect is that
they

they fhould improve upon all that has been per-
petrated by their predeceffors, and feverely realize
the foolifh vaunts of a foolifh king : " My little
finger fhall be thicker than my father's loins :
for whereas my father put a heavy yoke upon you,
I will put more to your yoke ; my father chaf-
tized you with whips, but I will chaftize you
with fcorpions."

MARIUS.

LET-

LETTER VIII.

To EDMUND BURKE, Esq.

SIR,

IF, in the present distracted state of this country, the freedom with which I have considered the conduct of our representatives required
an apology, I could use no better one than a
quotation from your own celebrated Speech :
" They must grant to me, in my turn, that all
political power which is set over men, and that
all privilege claimed or exercised in exclusion
of them, being wholly artificial, and, for so
much, a derogation from the natural equality of
mankind at large, ought to be some way or
other exercised ultimately for their benefit."

" If this is true with regard to every species
of political dominion, and every description of
commercial privilege, none of which can be
original self-derived rights, or grants for the
more private benefit of the holders, then such
rights or privileges, or whatever else you choose
to call them, are all in the strictest sense a *trust* ;
and it is of the very essence of every trust to be

N   rendered

rendered *accountable* ; and even totally to *ceafe*, when it fubftantially varies from the purpofes for which alone it could have a lawful ex- iftence *."

I have confidered, in my former letter, not fo much the pretended abufes in the adminiftra- tion of our Eaft-Indian poffeffions, of which I confefs myfelf no adequate judge, (though I do not believe nine tenths of your own honorable houfe more qualified for the decifion,) as the me- thod of eftablifhing them, and the jurifdiction of the tribunal before which they are brought. I have attempted to prove, that, in the whole

---

* Speech, p. 7.—This extraordinary confeffion puts me in mind of the following ftory, to be found, I believe, in Pilpay's Fables. A certain man, very uxcrioufly inclined, had a young and beautiful wife, who always treated him with the moft open averfion and difdain ; till one night, fpy- ing a thief in the room, fhe took refuge in the arms of her hufband, who was afleep, with fuch unufual fondnefs as awakened him. But when the good-man learned the caufe of her terrors, he called out in raptures to the thief, who had been alarmed and was moving off, " Pray, fir, ftay ! the happinefs you have procured me is fo great that you are wel- come to all I have in return."—This condefcenfion in their reprefentatives is certainly as new to the people of England as was the fondnefs of the wife to the poor doating hufband; but they do not feem equally grateful : or have they already given fo much, that they have no more to beftow ?

proceeding,

proceeding, nothing is to be found worthy the gravity, dignity, or difintereftednefs of a Britifh fenate ; that nothing could be a greater mockery of all ideas of right and juftice, than that the fame perfons fhould fit in judgment upon the validity of their own engagments, who had contracted them originally, and ratified them at repeated intervals ; that, if the honorable houfe pretended to fit as a court of juftice, it has not obferved a fingle rule or decorum which could convince the nation of its impartiality ; not even the flimfy forms and punctilios which attended the quo warrantos of the laft century, or the condemnations of Sydney and Ruffel. It was a fpecies of fummary juftice which improves upon Afiatic models, and will afford inftructions to each fucceeding Jefferies for ages. But another confideration equally important remains : fuppofing the houfe of commons had been a tribunal ever fo well adapted to the enquiry, fuppofing the guilt of the Eaft-India company to have been ever fo clearly proved, what is the nature of the remedy propofed for thefe diforders, and what the benefit which we may fairly expect from its adminiftration ? For even if all the abufe, which the invention of intereft and malice combined have heaped together, fhould be admitted, it will not follow that the propofed remedy is adapt-

ed

ed to remove the evil, or even to palliate its moſt alarming ſymptoms. This examination, ſir, will furniſh a proper comment for your ſpeech, and may fill up ſome chaſms which I have obſerved between the premiſes and the concluſions.

For even ſuppoſing certain abuſes ſhould have been clearly proved to exiſt in the adminiſtration of the Eaſt India Company's affairs, ſhould thoſe abuſes alſo be of ſufficient magnitude to juſtify the interference of parliament, it will by no means follow, that Mr. Fox's pretended bill of reform was either neceſſary, or adapted to the purpoſe. But in order to make this ariſe as an inevitable concluſion, you aſſume the ſtrangeſt ſeries of facts that I believe was ever obtruded npon the public. For firſt you conclude " that this body (meaning the whole body of proprietors), being totally perverted from the purpoſes of its inſtitution, is utterly incorrigible ; and becauſe they are incorrigible, both in conduct and conſtitution, power ought to be taken out of their hands : juſt on the ſame principles on which have been made all the juſt changes and revolutions of government that have taken place ſince the beginning of the world."＊ To aſſume that any body of people is not only corrupted, but incorrigible, is, to a plain and common underſtanding, one of the moſt ex

traordinary

＊ Speech, p. 88.

traordinary pofitions that I think was ever ven-
tured in a ferious publication. It fhould feem,
fir, that you hold the doctrine of free-will in
fo entire and abfolute a manner, that you leave
no room for the application of new motives to
the mind ; or elfe you fall into the contrary
extreme, and affert that the conduct will remain
the fame, though every principle of action
fhould be changed. Choofe which you will of
thefe abfurdities ; for they are both before you.
Nor is it a common fpecies of corruption alone
of which they are accufed, fuch as fome ignorant
people have attributed to a virtuous majority, the
preferring their private to the public intereft ;
but the more extraordinary one of not only being
incapable of regulating their own affairs, but of
becoming fo by any procefs that can be operated
even by the omnipotence of parliament. Yet
this incorrigible body is compofed upon the
fame principles with the Bank, or any other public company that has ever exifted ; comprehends many hundred individuals, among whom
may be numbered the principal gentry of the
kingdom, and the moft opulent merchants of
the city of London.

I fhould imagine, fir, that were a foreigner, totally unverfed in the party hiftory of this kingdom, to hear fo extraordinary an affertion, he
would

would neceffarily imagine that the whole preceding hiftory of the Eaft-India company contained
nothing but the detail of public frauds and private blunders : more efpecially, when he reflected
upon the repeated generofity which had been
ufed in an arbitrary government, like that of
France, to fupport a fimilar eftablifhment, he
would conclude that the national affiftance and
generofity here muft have been fo repeatedly
abufed as to leave no farther room for pardon or
experiment. Neceffity, he would obferve, may
indeed juftify, as it occafions every attempt;
but it muft be a very uncommon kind of neceffity that can induce the government of a free
ftate to defert all its ufual principles, and to ufe
a difcretionary authority with greater rigour
than was ever known in an arbitrary one. But
what would be his aftonifhment, when he was
told the real hiftory of this oppreft and perfe-
cuted company ? That, incorrigible as it is now
reprefented to be, and radically corrupted, it had,
by its own exertions, obtained a degree of greatnefs perhaps unparalleled in the hiftory of the
world. That its commerce, while it poured into
the bofom of the mother-country all the varied
productions of the fruitful Eaft, had afforded
fuch ample fupplies to its revenue as would alone
fupport the expences of a moderate ftate. That its

prefent

prefent diftreffes were chiefly the temporary effects
of a ruinous and inevitable war, in which it had
been involved by the ambition of thofe very patriots who now exult with a malignant joy over
the wounds which they have occafioned, and,
inftead of binding them up, are haftening to
draw forth the vital fluids by the orifice. Its
own refources, it would be added, have nurfed
it up to a degree of power and opulence which
awes one portion of the globe, while it excites
the envy of all the reft. Although originally
intended for commerce alone, it has gradually
extended its power and influence, till it has involved the fates of mighty empires, and attracted
them to itfelf. Whatever may be now advanced, by intereft or malevolence,, about
the crimes and incapacity of its fervants, is
amply confuted even by the unexaggerated
detail of events. What ftronger evidence can
be given of the folid bafis upon which any human
power is founded, than its capacity to refift and
triumph over the mightieft attacks ? This, even
exclufively, is the boaft of the Englifh Eaft-
India company. With every difadvantage of
difficulty and diftance, it has prevailed, not only
over the feeble oppofition of Afiatic princes, but
over all the efforts of one of the moft politic and
warlike nations in the univerfe. Could this have
been effected without a fpirit, both of counfel,
and

and of enterprife ?—No—whatever may be the reprefentations of parliamentary orators, the world at large will refute the wild and chimerial accufation. Whatever may be the demerits of the company, whatever the catalogue of its crimes, the comparative feries of its minifters may certainly vie with that of any modern government of Europe. It has undoubtedly produced warriors of intrepid minds and heroes of immortal fame ; chiefs that have dared, in their employers and country's caufe, all that men can dare ; that have executed every thing which the prefent colleagues of Mr. Burke have *failed* to do. Even now, " on evil days though fall'n, and evil tongues," it can boaft of characters that would do honour to any nation ; the foremoft of whom is that very culprit, that feems fingly, like an electric rod upon a noble edifice, to have protected the building beneath, while he attracts the fury of the tempeft upon himfelf. Yet even he, " fcathed," as he may appear, by all the lightnings of parliamentary vengeance, nor afks the mercy, nor deprecates the rage of his accufers : he is ready to leave the throne of half the Eaft in order to meet their impeachments ; he bids them take his life, if any thing worthy of death fhall be found in his conduct ; nor dare his moft inveterate enemies accept the offer.

Is

Is this, fir, the language of party or cabal?
If it be, I wifh it were oftener heard within the
walls of even your own virtuous houfe. It is the
voice of a man who is equally unacquainted
with Mr. Haftings and his friends; totally un-
connected with the affairs and interefts of the
Eaft-India company. It is the voice of a man
who has never been feen at the levees of either
your friends or antagonifts; who has never flat-
tered even the people, much as he loves them,
in their delufions, or cringed to them for their
fupport. But it is the voice of an independent
man, that dares to exprefs his fentiments in defiance of the moft powerful faction of this country, and that has a character to hazard upon the
ftake. As to Mr. Haftings, his abilities are fo
undoubted, and there is fo ftrong an impreffion
of a great and noble ambition in all his actions,
that I cannot help admiring him; and that admiration, I confefs, makes me ready to efteem
him: I am interefted in his fate, and wifh to
find that he has added the praife of integrity to
that of a comprehenfive underftanding and elevated mind. If ever there was an individual
who deferved to have the weaknefles or defects of
human nature overfhadowed by his triumphs,
it certainly is Mr. Haftings; yet, were his
achievements and his qualities ten times greater

O   than

than they are, I never would interpofe to fcreen him from public juftice, if he has deferved it; on the contrary, I would be the firft to mount the roftrum, and arreft him in his triumphal pro-grefs, did I live in a country where any punifh-ments were inflicted upon public guilt, or where private virtue might direct the vengeance of the nation. But fuch as he is, he does not deferve to fall unheard. His fate fhould be an honorable wound, in fair and equal battle; not to be trodden down by a bafe and promifcuous rabble that are only ftruggling for his fpoils. Let him fall hereafter, a victim to the offended genius of Afia, and to the infulted juftice of his country; but let him, while he lives, enjoy the honors and the veneration of an hero. His death, whenever it arrives, will neither difgrace his friends, nor be unworthy of himfelf; it will be folemn and lamented, the cataftrophe of an awful drama: juftice will be expiated and forrow for the ftroke; it will not refufe the confolation of an honorable interment, or deny a martial trophy to adorn his tomb: it is envy alone that would fteal the noble corpfe, and hew it out to glut the fury of parliamentary hounds*.

This,

* There are two circumftances effential to every free ftate; that no individual fhould either be elevated beyond the reach of public juftice, or condemned unheard. No-thing can be a furer prefage of approaching ruin to fuch a

ftate

This, fir, like many parts of your own
Speech, is declamation ; but it is not, as they
are,

ftate than that degree of power which fruftrates all enquiry,
or that degree of violence which tramples upon the falutary
forms of criminal inveftigation. The more enormous is the
imputed guilt, the more cautious fhould we be in examining whether it really exift. An unfortunate man, not very
long ago, fell a victim to the odium which had been ex-
cited by the atrocious nature of the crime alleged againft
him ; and this muft fometimes happen, in fpite of the moft
excellent fyftem of criminal proceedings that any country
could ever boaft. How cautious then ought we to be in
pronouncing upon the guilt of thofe who are abfent, and
where the fcene of accufation lies in another hemifphere!
I am very ill qualified to decide concerning the merit of
Mr. Haftings; but I am fufficiently qualified to pronounce
that not one of the charges againft him has yet been proved
to the fatisfaction of any impartial man : nor is there one
of them which has not been denied, and very forcibly, at
leaft very fpecioufly, invalidated. Mr. Burke, in the fer-
vour of his complimental eloquence, has this paffage (p. 81):
" This man, whofe deep reach of thought, whofe large
legiflative conceptions, and whofe grand plans of policy,
make the moft fhining part of our reports, *from whence we
have all learned our leffions, if we have learned any good ones*;
this man, from whofe materials thofe gentlemen who have
leaft acknowledged it, have yet fpoken as from a brief," &c.
This paffage, I muft confefs, appears to me a very unfortunate one ; fince it feems to place the foundation of all
the bitter charges, both againft Mr. Haftings and the Eaft-
India company, upon the evidence and reprefentations of
one gentleman alone, and that gentleman known to have
been upon terms of perfonal enmity with the parties accufed. Whatever may be the integrity and abilities of any

man,

are, unfupported by fact or argument. And
are the proprietors of the Eaft-India ftock to
be calumniated with every difgraceful epithet
that can fting the heart, or degrade the character
of man, merely becaufe they did not recall a
minifter like Mr. Haftings, at the inftigation of
what now compofes a majority of the commons?
On the contrary, it would have been madnefs
to have done it; and it is the ftrongeft proof
both of their underftanding and their independence, that they have dared to difregard the idle
thunders of fuch a vote, and to follow the
dictates of their own better fenfe. Yet, that
they have dared to do this, and to maintain the
freedom of their own appointments, in oppofition to the fenfe of the committees of the
houfe of commons, is a fufficient reafon for
your declaring " that the condition of the company is incorrigible." Strange logic indeed!
and a new fpecies of dilemma! Either the whole
corporation is at once to refign its legal powers

man, common juftice requires that allowance fhould be
made for thofe paffions which are infeparable from human
nature: nor are fuch accufations as are produced in the
Speech I allude to, to be admitted upon the teftimony of
any individual in the univerfe ; ftill lefs upon another perfon's reprefentation, even of that very teftimony. For
Mr. Burke himfelf allows, *that he has learned his leffon,*
without producing his mafter.

into

into the hands of a majority of the houfe, to
change the tenour of its proceedings, difplace
its fervants, and manage its commercial affairs
by every caprice of men, who, whatever they
may know, can know but little of India
affairs, or elfe the punifhment of this *audacity* *
is to be the confifcation of all their privileges,
and the forfeiture of all their property. I have
heard of an highwayman, that prefented a
piftol to a gentleman's breaft with this apoftro-
phe, " Sir, give me all your money, or elfe
by G—d you'll be robbed." I will not pain
your delicacy by the application of the ftory;
but will you pleafe to inform us, where was the
crime of the proprietors refifting a vote of the
houfe ? If it be a crime, why are they not proceeded againft and punifhed in a legal way?
But if it be no more a crime for them to perfift
in maintaining their own appointment, than
it would be in me to keep a footman in defiance
of a vote of the houfe of commons, how can
this eftablifh either their corruption or their in-
corrigibility ?

But let me be permitted to analyze your
Speech, and, throwing the pomp of metaphor

---

* " Ever fince the beginning of this feffion, the fame
act of audacity was repeated."—P. 87.

and

and allufion afide, to confider the fimple facts
and arguments which it contains. Neither
you, nor any of your honorable friends, can
deny that the Eaft-India company have, for a
confiderable fpace of time previous to thefe accufations, managed their affairs with confiderable attention and ability. Their profperity
is a fufficient proof of this and the ftability of
their empire. Now, fir, the whole period which
is contained in your accufations fcarcely extends
to a dozen years. You were their defender in
the year 1769, if you are the author of the
pamphlet called, " Obfervations on a late State
of the Nation ;" and you have defended them
as low as the year 1781, if any faith is to be
given to the parliamentary Debates. Even in
your prefent Speech you unguardedly allow
" the fact is, that for a long time there was a
ftruggle, a faint one, indeed, between the company and their fervants *; of the directors you
affirm, " there have been, fir, very frequently,
men of the greateft integrity and virtue amongft
them † :" yet, after having paraded through
an hundred pages of mere declamation and
vague accufations, which have been repeatedly
anfwered and contradicted, you gravely con-

* Speech, p. 88.   † Ibid. p. 83.

clude

clude that the whole body both of proprietors
and directors is utterly incorrigible; the one
for oppofing the vote of parliament; the other,
I fuppofe, for yielding obedience to it *. I
believe fuch a conclufion derived from fuch
premifes was never before hazarded by a man
of your abilities: for what can be inferred even
after the moft implicit acquiefcence in all your
charges, not one of which has been authenti-
cated, unlefs that the fervants of the company
have for fome years paft been guilty of mif-
behaviour, and that the proprietors, piqued,
according to your own account †, by the interference

" * The directors, ftill retaining fome fhadow of refpect to
this houfe, inftituted an enquiry themfelves, which continued from June to October ; and, after an attentive perufal
and full confideration of papers, refolved to take fteps for
removing the perfons who had been the objects of our
refolutions."—Speech, p. 86.—Yet, p. 89, the directors
themfelves are all wolves. " He would appoint the wolf a
guardian of the fheep; but he has invented a curious
muzzle, by which this protecting wolf fhall not be able to
open his jaws above an inch or two at the utmoft."

May it not be afked whether any perfon was ever more
conftantly reprefented in the light of a wolf, than Lord
North by Mr. Burke and all his friends ?—Yet a late
tranfaction is a proof that wolves may either change their
nature, or be moft happily reftrained from mifchief, by
means of a *coalition muzzle.*

† " Even the attempt you have made to enquire into
their practices, and to reform abufes, has raifed and piqued
them

terference of the commons, have not fhewn all due refpect to their illuftrious vote?

But why muft they be for this reafon incorrigible? Is not every body of men fubject to errors and to paffions? Do not a calmer confideration of affairs, and longer experience, frequently point out the neceffity of an alteration of conduct? And why might not the fame revolution of things take place in refpect to them, which we have feen exemplified in the houfe of commons? For almoft twenty years, fir, the nation has heard you and your friends declaiming againft venality and fecret influence; for almoft twenty years, if we can believe your reprefentations, there has been fcarcely a meafure which has not begun in folly and terminated in wickednefs. This is a longer fpace of reprobation than what you have alleged againft the Eaft-India company. Yet fee how time, in its filent progrefs, accomplifhes the moft ftupendous revolutions! This houfe, which formerly was a den of thieves, is now become the temple of the Lord; " an independent houfe of

them to a far more regular and fteady fupport."—Speech, p. 88.—May it not be fufpected that refentment againft an interference, which they juftly thought improper, might act upon the minds of the proprietors, as much as this original fin of corruption?

commons;

commons; an houfe of commons which has, by
its own virtue, deftroyed the influence of parliamentary fubferviency." †

But as to the idea of any body of men, that
is in a continual ftate of fluctuation, being
incurably and neceffarily corrupt, the idea is as
unphilofophical as the purpofe for which it is
introduced is unjuft. Is it for me, fir, to inform a man, that infifts fo frequently and with
fo much pleafure upon his acquaintance with
mankind, that every body of men is acted upon
by circumftances, and changes its character in
unifon with the general changes which furround
it? Even parliaments have been difinterefted
and defended the liberties of the people. If
they are grown indifferent to thefe circumftances, it is becaufe the general relaxation of
the times admits the depravity; and becaufe
faction and intrigue have been difcovered to be
more effectual ways of making a fortune than
virtue or integrity. But fhould the people once
more rouze from their lethargy, and demand a
fevere account from their reprefentatives, of
all the millions which they have fquandered, of
all the mifmanagement which they have con-
nived at; fhould they for the future infift upon
private virtue and public confiftency as indif-

† Speech, p. 97.
P.   penfable

penfable qualifications, we might perhaps fee a change more extraordinary, in a certain honorable houfe, than any which mark the year 1783.

But as to the defencelefs proprietors of Eaft-India ftock, it is an equal reflection upon your houfe to have fuffered their crimes and obftinacy fo long as you pretend, and to be incapable of correcting it now. All men, in every fituation, are naturally guided by the impulfe of their own intereft; nor does a government ever depend upon the virtue of its fubjects, but upon the wifdom of its own regulations. It afcertains the crime, it fixes the mode of profecution, it eftablifhes the penalty. Look, I pray you, fir, at your own ftatutes; there you will find a thoufand of the moft innocent actions in life prohibited under the fevereft penalties. Men may not confume the product of their own fields, they may not fee the light of heaven, they may not fteep an handful of barley-corns in water, without the leave of government. Lately you have undertaken that no man fhall difcharge the duties of common honefty, that not a labourer fhall pay his ale-houfe fcore, without the interference of government; and rather than fail, you hold out an univerfal patronage to every villain throughout the kingdom. Do you imagine, fir, that men fubmit

willingly

willingly and chearfully to thefe abfurd op-
preffions ? No ; they curfe your parties and
your politics *in every tongue,* by every *form of
religion,* which prevails throughout the empire.
But hard neceffity compels, the iron hand of
power, and the terrors of impending punifhment. Are you able to do all this, and are you
obliged to yield to the obftinacy alone of India proprietors ; men that are chained down in the midft
of the capital ; who are every inftant expofed to
your power, and obnoxious to your vengeance ;
whofe fortunes are the conftant pledges of their
conduct, and expofed, if they difobey, to all
your confcientious encroachments ? But pardon
me, fir, if I tell you that the whole fcheme is
fuch a chaos of abfurdity, bad reafoning, and
oppreffion, as never before difgraced a government.

Men will certainly neither yield up their property or their liberty to the pretended neceffities
of government, fo long as they can retain them.
But are the reports of the committees to enquire
into the frauds practifed upon the revenue, a
fufficient reafon to pronounce that the brewers,
the diftillers, and the numerous other traders
who are now the daily victims of the excife,
are become incorrigible ; and therefore to inveft
their fhops, their warehoufes, their diftilleries,

in

in parliamentary commiſſioners? Yet the principle is equally applicable; with this difference
only, that after ſome hundred pages of declamation, not a ſingle action has been proved againſt
the Eaſt-India proprietors, which does not ſpring
from their undoubted right.

But from the firſt ill-omened hour, the year
1767*, when the affairs of the company were

* It is worth while to conſider the following account of
that tranſaction.—"The Eaſt-India company had for a
good while ſolicited the miniſtry for a negociation, by
which they propoſed to pay largely for ſome advantages in
their trade, and for the renewal of their charter. This had
been the former method of tranſacting with that body.
Government having only leaſed the monopoly for ſhort
terms, the company has been obliged to reſort to it
frequently for renewals. Theſe two parties had always ne-
gociated (on the true principle of credit) not as government
and ſubject, but as equal dealers, on the footing of mutual
advantage. The public had derived great benefit from ſuch
dealing. But at that time new ideas prevailed," &c. &c.—
See the curious paſſage at length in a pamphlet called,
" Obſervations on a late State of the Nation," p. 89.
The following perhaps may not be inapplicable to the
preſent times. " In conſequence of this ſcheme, the terrors of a parliamentary enquiry were hung over them. A
judicature was aſſerted in parliament to try this queſtion.
But, leſt this judicial character ſhould chance to inſpire certain ſtubborn ideas of law right, it was argued, that the
judicature was arbitrary, and ought not to determine by the
rules of law, but by their opinion of policy and expedi-
ency. Nothing exceeded the violence of ſome of the ma-
nagers, except their impatience. They were bewildered
by their paſſions, and by their want of knowledge, or want
of conſideration of the ſubject."—Ibid, p. 90.

expoſed

expofed to the prophane and licentious eyes of
the houfe, it was eafy to forefee how the interference would end, and what was the reformation intended. Neither faith, nor gratitude,
nor promifes, can bind the rapacity of minifters and their virtuous majorities. In vain might
the company plead their merits with the country;
the numerous advantages which it continually
derived from their commerce; the millions with
which it had enriched the public revenue beyond example, almoft beyond calculation ! when
once a government is thoroughly corrupted,
wealth and profperity are crimes againft the ftate,
and the name of private right or franchife becomes rebellion. The fpirit of defpotifm is
blind as it is intolerant, and the nobleft trees of
the foreft muft fall, to fave the trouble of
gathering the fruit.

This, and not the defire of reformation, has,
I fear, guided all the invafions which have been
made upon the company's rights; from the
famous bill which prevented their fending over
fupervifors † to examine and correct the ftate of
their affairs, down to the prefent, which punifhes
them for the omiffion, by the confifcation of all
their property. To diftract their counfels, and

---

† In the year 1772.

embarrafs

embarrafs their affairs; to continue every abufe, but fruftrate every plan of reformation, till loaded with a weight of public odium and private diftreffes, they might fink for ever into the bottomlefs gulf of minifterial influence; has this, fir, been, or has it not, the uniform, undeviating policy of government ?—While you paufe upon this important queftion, I will take my leave of you for the prefent, with the intention of renewing our correfpondence.

MARIUS.

FINIS.